LAW & GRACE

An Expository Study in the Rudiments of Sin and Truth

CHARLES MWEWA

Republished by:

AFRICA IN CANADA PRESS (ACP)
Ottawa, Ontario
Canada
acpress.ca
charlesmwewa.com

Copyright © 2023 Charles Mwewa

All rights reserved.

ISBN-13: 978-1-988251-42-4

Dedication

For

Cuteravive

Table of Contents

Dedication iii

Table of Contents v

Table of Verses xi

Introduction xvii

    Sin and Truth xvii

    In Summary xxiv

1 | LAW 1

    Varieties of Laws: Law of Men 1

    Varieties of Laws: Law of God 3

    The Significance of Law 15

    In Summary 17

2 | GRACE 19

    Meaning of Grace 19

    Salvation: Grace and Faith 22

    In Summary 25

3 | THREE UNCHANGING TRUTHS 27

    Sin, Conscience and Salvation 27

Salvation Neutralizes Sin's Power.................27

The Umpire of Conscience............................29

True Salvation Is Never Lost 36

In Summary..44

4 | EIGHT PRINCIPLES OF GRACE.........45

1. Love is Refined...45

2. Work is Redefined...................................45

3. Boldness to Enter....................................46

4. Love before Commitment 47

5. Lost But Found 52

6. Grace Supersedes Law............................63

7. In-Christ Sinless Perfection 74

8. A Sealed Inheritance 80

In Summary..86

5 | THE FAITH FACTOR...............................95

Faith – An Only Channel to Spiritual Blessings..95

Christ Died; Believers Died 97

The Holy Spirit Guarantees the Inheritance
....99

The Three Premises 101

In Conclusion 105

6 | GOSPEL AND GRACE 107

Grace Saves 107

The Sin Dilemma 110

The Beauty of the Gospel............................. 115

The Power of the Gospel – It's Free 120

Communicating Grace 125

In Summary... 126

7 | JEW AND GENTILE UNDER GRACE
.... 129

Favor from Favoritism................................. 129

Ten Ways in Which Grace Increases 132

In Summary... 137

8 | FAVOR 139

Principle.. 139

Prototypical Factor 141

Conditional Factor 143

Reiteratory Factor 145

Beauty 148

Ten Characteristics of a Blessing from God 148

In Summary 152

9 | GRACE AND TITHING 155

Tithing in Pre-Law Period 155

Tithing during the Law Period 156

Classes of Tithing 166

No Tithing in New Testament 168

Grace, Tithing and the New Testament ... 189

In Summary 208

10 | PRAYER AND GRACE 209

The Old Meets the New 209

In Summary 217

11 | TEN BENEFITS OF GRACE 223

In Summary 226

12 | GRACE AND DISCIPLINE 229

Grace in the Disciplinary Process 229

Natural Justice 233

Alternative Dispute Resolution (ADR) 234

Disciplinary Process 237

In Summary..244

13 | GOVERNMENT, LAW AND GRACE
....245

    Ultimate Role of Government....................248

    Four Core Values of Government.............250

    Law and Core Values...................................253

    Grace and Core Values 257

    In Summary..262

ABOUT THE AUTHOR.................................265

INDEX..267

Table of Verses

1 Chronicles 21:16	Exodus 33:12-14	Matthew 23:23
1 Chronicles 29:14, 16	Ezekiel 18:20a	Matthew 24:13-14
1 Corinthians 1:30	Ezekiel 27:31	Matthew 25:41
1 Corinthians 1:4	Ezra 9:8	Matthew 26:39
1 Corinthians 1:5	Galatians 1:6	Matthew 3:9
1 Corinthians 10:13	Galatians 1:8	Matthew 5:17-18
1 Corinthians 10:23	Galatians 2:16	Matthew 5:23-25
1 Corinthians 10:26	Galatians 3:24	Matthew 5:38-39
1 Corinthians 10:31	Galatians 3:25	Matthew 5:44-45
1 Corinthians 11:29-31	Galatians 3:6	Matthew 5:48
1 Corinthians 14:20	Galatians 4:19	Matthew 5:5
1 Corinthians 15:10	Galatians 4:4-5	Matthew 6:10b
1 Corinthians 15:35-58	Galatians 5:1	Matthew 6:16-17
1 Corinthians 15:41	Galatians 5:3-4	Matthew 6:19-21
1 Corinthians 2:6	Galatians 6:6	Matthew 6:33
1 Corinthians 3:10	Genesis 1: 14-19	Matthew 6:9
1 Corinthians 3:15	Genesis 1:25	Matthew 7:1
1 Corinthians 4:12	Genesis 14:18-20	Matthew 7:12
1 Corinthians 5:1-5	Genesis 15:6	Matthew 7:7

1 Corinthians 6:12	Genesis 19:19	Matthew 8:3-4
1 Corinthians 6:19	Genesis 2:16-17	Micah 6:8
1 Corinthians 9:11-14	Genesis 24:35	Nehemiah 9:1
1 John 1:8	Genesis 26:12	Number 18: 20-24
1 John 1:9	Genesis 28:20–22	Numbers 18:26
1 John 2:19	Genesis 32:5	Numbers 22:28
1 John 3:19-21	Genesis 33:10	Numbers 32:5
1 John 3:20-22	Genesis 33:15	Philippians 1:7
1 John 3:4b	Genesis 33:8	Philippians 2:13
1 John 3:5	Genesis 34:11	Philippians 3:12
1 John 3:9	Genesis 37:34	Philippians 2:6-8
1 John 4:19	Genesis 39:4	Philippians 2:8
1 John 4:8	Genesis 4:9	Philippians 3:12
1 Kings 21:27	Genesis 47:25	Philippians 4:6
1 Peter 1:19	Genesis 47:29	Philippians 4:8
1 Peter 2:9	Genesis 50:4	Proverbs 10:22
1 Peter 4: 10	Genesis 6:8	Proverbs 14:34
1 Peter 4:10-11	Genesis 8:22	Proverbs 21:3
1 Samuel 1:18	Haggai 2:8	Proverbs 22:11
1 Samuel 20:3	Hebrews 10:2	Proverbs 28:13
1 Samuel 27:5	Hebrews 11:1	Proverbs 3:22
1 Thessalonians 4:11-12	Hebrews 11:6	Proverbs 3:34
1 Thessalonians 4:14	Hebrews 12:15	Proverbs 3:9-10
1 Thessalonians 5:16-18	Hebrews 12:6	Proverbs 4:9
1 Thessalonians 5:17	Hebrews 13:9	Proverbs 8:21
1 Timothy 2:2	Hebrews 2:17	Psalm 11:7
1 Timothy 2:8	Hebrews 4:15	Psalm 119: 89-120

1 Timothy 4:3	Hebrews 4:16	Psalm 119:142
1 Timothy 4:4-5	Hebrews 5:8-9	Psalm 127:1
1 Timothy 5:18	Hebrews 6:10	Psalm 14:1
1 Timothy 6:17	Hebrews 6:5-6	Psalm16:9–11
2 Chronicles 25	Hebrews 7:4-10	Romans 1:1-5
2 Corinthians 8:7	Hebrews 9:14	Romans 10:4
2 Corinthians 9:8	Hebrews 9:15	Romans 10:9
2 Corinthians 11:8-9	Isaiah 1:17	Romans 11:4
2 Corinthians 12:10	Isaiah 15:3	Romans 11:6
2 Corinthians 12:13-15	Isaiah 26:10	Romans 12:1-2
2 Corinthians 12:7-10	Isaiah 40:6	Romans 13:1-7
2 Corinthians 4:15	Isaiah 42:5	Romans 13:8-10
2 Corinthians 5:17-21	Isaiah 52:7	Romans 14:15
2 Corinthians 5:19	Isaiah 53:2	Romans 14:22
2 Corinthians 5:21	Isaiah 64:6	Romans 14:23
2 Corinthians 8:12-14	James 1:17	Romans 14:6
2 Corinthians 8:7	James 2:13b	Romans 15:26
2 Corinthians 8:9	James 4:17	Romans 15:27
2 Corinthians 9:1-8	James 4:6	Romans 2:11
2 Corinthians 9:7	Jeremiah 29:7	Romans 3:20-24
2 Corinthians 9:8	Jeremiah 31:2	Romans 3:20b
2 Peter 1:2	Jeremiah 31:33b	Romans 3:21-22
2 Peter 1:3-4	Jeremiah 49:3	Romans 3:23
2 Peter 3:9	Job 16:15	Romans 3:24
2 Samuel 14:22	John 1:14	Romans 3:24-26
2 Samuel 16:4	John 1:16-17	Romans 3:28
2 Samuel 3:31	John 10:10	Romans 4:15
2 Thessalonians	John 16:11	Romans 4:16

3: 6-11

2 Timothy 1:10	John 16:8	Romans 4:22-25
2 Timothy 1:7	John 17:24	Romans 5:20
2 Timothy 1:9	John 18:38	Romans 5:8
2 Timothy 2:1	John 3:16	Romans 6:1-2
2 Timothy 3:16	John 3:36	Romans 6:14
2 Timothy 4:22	John 6:29	Romans 6:18
Acts 10:34-36	John 6:37	Romans 6:6
Acts 11:23	John 8:3-11	Romans 7:13-14
Acts 11:27-28	John 8:31-32	Romans 7:18-20
Acts 15:11	John 8:46	Romans 7:22-23
Acts 16:31	John 8:5	Romans 7:6
Acts 17:24	John 8:7	Romans 7:7
Acts 20:33-35	Jonah 3:5-9	Romans 7:8-11
Acts 20:24	Judges 21:25	Romans 8: 1 and 2
Acts 20:32-35	Judges 6:17	Romans 8:17
Acts 4: 36-37	Lamentations 2:10	Romans 8:18
Acts 6:8	Lamentations 3:22-23	Romans 8:28
Acts 8:20	Leviticus 13 – 16	Romans 8:3
Colossians 1:14	Leviticus 19:15	Romans 8:32
Colossians 1:6	Leviticus 19:18	Titus 2:11-13
Colossians 3:17	Leviticus 24:19–21	Zechariah 11:10
Daniel 1:15	Leviticus 27: 31-34	Zechariah 11:7
Daniel 2:21	Luke 11:42	Zechariah 14:21
Deuteronomy 1:13	Luke 12:20-21	
Deuteronomy 12:5-6	Luke 12:32	
Deuteronomy 14:22	Luke 14:16-24	
Deuteronomy	Luke 15:11–32	

27:26	
Deuteronomy 28	Luke 16:10-11
Deuteronomy 28:2	Luke 16:8
Deuteronomy 4	Luke 18:1
Deuteronomy 8:18	Luke 18:12
Ephesians 1:15-16	Luke 4:18
Ephesians 1:17	Malachi 3:10-11
Ephesians 1:3, 13-14	Malachi 3:6a
Ephesians1:7	Malachi 3:8
Ephesians 2:8	Malachi 3:9
Ephesians 2:8-10	Mark 12:31
Ephesians 3:19-21	Mark 12:43-44
Ephesians 3:2	Matthew 10:8
Ephesians 3:7	Matthew 11:21
Ephesians 3:8	Matthew 12:45
Ephesians 4:13	Matthew 13:19
Ephesians 4:7	Matthew 17:20
Esther 2:16-17	Matthew 20:1-16
Exodus 20:1-17	Exodus 33:12-14
Exodus 21	Ezekiel 18:20a
Exodus 25–31 and 35–40	Ezekiel 27:31
	Ezra 9:8

Introduction

Sin and Truth

Law defines sin. Without a law to break, there can be no sin: "Everyone who sins breaks God's law, because sin is the same as breaking God's law."[1] From the very beginning, according to the Bible, God set a law in the Garden of Eden. The law, with its attendant penalty, was set in Genesis: "And the LORD God commanded him, 'You may eat freely from every tree of the garden, but you must not eat from the tree of the knowledge of good and evil; for in the day that you eat of it, you will surely die.'"[2] The first law proscribed against eating from the tree of the knowledge of good and evil. The penalty was physical and spiritual death. Humanity has lived with this penalty to date. People die because the law was broken.

The law is not bad in itself. However, without the law, sin could not have existed. "What shall we say, then? Is the law sinful? Certainly not! Nevertheless, I would not have known what sin was had it not been

---

[1] 1 John 3:4, (Contemporary English Version)
[2] Genesis 2:16-17

for the law. For I would not have known what coveting really was if the law had not said, 'You shall not covet.'"[3] Good as it may be, the law is responsible for all sins. We know what sin is because the law defined it and is the essence of its enforcement.

The law brings the awareness of sin. The law tells us that there is sin: "For the law merely brings awareness of sin."[4] The simple truth is that if law is eliminated, so will be sin. The law introduces sin, and with-it, God's wrath. If there is no law, there will be no sin: "because the law brings wrath. And where there is no law, there is no transgression."[5]

This is a universal postulation. Consider the laws of men. If the regulator does not proscribe parking in a certain location at a certain time, no motorist would be breaking the law by parking there. Or if the law did not say that homicide is murder, no one would be committing murder by killing another human being. Or still, if the law did not say that stealing is sin, in the same way no one would be called a thief if they stole from another person. If there are no commandments, there would be no law to break, and therefore, no sin to commit.

There would be no sinners if there were no laws, commandments or injunctions to contravene. Just like an offense, a tort, or a

---

[3] Romans 7:7
[4] Romans 3:20b
[5] Romans 4:15

crime is a contravention of the law, so sin is the transgression of God's law.

Behavior is neither moral nor immoral unless there is a law against it. And the dilemma under the law is that there are many laws in place – ceremonial, liturgical, canonical, divine, or the *Decalogue* (Ten Commandments) and many more. It is, therefore, almost impossible not to be a sinner. For when one would be obeying one set of laws, they might be disobeying another set in the same act.

Humanity is born under the penalty of sin, and, therefore, is guilty of the breach of the first law. Thus, "For all have sinned, and fall short of the glory of God."[6] For humans, even before their birth, they had been fashioned in sin: "Behold, I was sharpen in iniquity; and in sin did my mother conceive me."[7]

Humans sin not because they can avoid it, but because they cannot. Their very nature is of sin – they have a sinful nature from birth. No one explicitly trains a child to sin; it sins simply. How did the child know how to lie, steal and be violent? It was by natural urge. The child simply lied, stole and became violent. Thankfully, the Bible has exposed this truth.

Humans are born with an evil nature. And no matter how good intentioned they

---

[6] Romans 3:23
[7] Psalm 51:5

are, their nature draws them into doing bad: "I know that nothing good lives in me, that is, in my flesh; for I have the desire to do what is good, but I cannot carry it out. For I do not do the good I want to do. Instead, I keep on doing the evil I do not want to do. And if I do what I do not want, it is no longer I who do it, but it is sin living in me that does it."[8] Therefore, the knowledge of good does not obviate the knowledge and penchant for doing evil. This condition was set in motion when humans violated the first order, the first law.

The only solution not to sin is to live without the law. This so-called Grace regime was inaugurated at the death and resurrection of Christ Jesus. Since then, the law is only persuasive, it is not binding upon believers: "For sin shall no longer be your master, because you are not under the law, but under grace."[9] As rendered in this verse of Scripture, sin is no longer our master; it was when we lived under the law. Under Grace, in principle, there is no law. It means just that; there is no law, except the Law of Grace itself, which is no law.

Under the Law of Grace, you are permitted to do anything. Yes, you read right, everything. In other words, everything is lawful under Grace. The rule is set in this verse: "'All things are lawful for me,' but

---

[8] Romans 7:18-20
[9] Romans 6:14

not all things are helpful. 'All things are lawful for me, but I will not be dominated by anything."[10] This rule is governed by the law of helpfulness (love) and freedom, and not fear and punishment. Thus, one should not murder because one loves their neighbor as they love themselves,[11] and likewise, "So in everything, do to others what you would have them do to you, for this sums up the Law and the Prophets."[12] Love, freedom and the Golden Rule should determine behavior under Grace, and not fear of sanctions.

While the strength of the law is sin, that of Grace is truth. Jesus came to bring both Grace and truth: "For the law was given through Moses; grace and truth came through Jesus Christ."[13] The truth (who is Jesus Christ) sets us free, and we are no longer slaves of sin. "It is for freedom that Christ has set us free. Stand firm, then, and do not let yourselves be burdened again by a yoke of slavery."[14] Believers in the Grace of God brought to us by Jesus Christ are no longer slaves of sin but slaves to righteousness: "You have been set free from sin and have become slaves to righteousness."[15] This injunction practically

---

[10] 1 Corinthians 6:12
[11] Mark 12:31
[12] Matthew 7:12
[13] John 1:17
[14] Galatians 5:1
[15] Romans 6:18

means that it is possible to live a righteous life under Grace, just as it was impossible to live a righteous life under law.

Under Grace, one can say anything, do anything, eat anything as long as it is helpful to them, loving to others and enforces freedom. This spiritual culture was prophesized many years before the birth of Jesus Christ: "I will put my law in their minds and write it on their hearts. I will be their God, and they will be my people."[16] And to ensure that this new law of Grace is self-enforceable, God has placed an awakened conscience in each of those who believe in Jesus Christ, "Whenever our conscience condemns us, we will be reassured that God is greater than our conscience and knows everything. Dear friends, if our conscience doesn't condemn us, we can boldly look to God and receive from him anything we ask. We receive it because we obey his commandments and do what pleases him."[17]

In other words, all the trimmings of the law have been contained under conscience. Conscience now dictates that we have kept God's commandments and have pleased Him even without doing a bit of an act. If conscience condemns us, it is merely directing us back into the path of Grace, or righteousness. When that happens, we

---

[16] Jeremiah 31:33b
[17] 1 John 3:20-22

confess[18] our sins and we are restored in an instant back into the realm of Grace and righteousness. Under Grace, we have a conscience of righteousness as our master, and not one of sin: "Otherwise, would they not have ceased being offered, because of those serving having been cleansed once, no longer having conscience of sins?[19]

And last comes the test for Grace, it is not works but faith. Everything under Grace must be of faith, otherwise anything done, said or planned without faith becomes traditional sin: "Whatever does not proceed from faith is sin."[20] Thus, to enjoy peace, righteousness, freedom, salvation and good things from God, under Grace, we need to access them all through faith. This is the lowest and best standard, because anyone can succeed under Grace. And that faith can be as little as a mustard seed: "He replied, 'Because you have so little faith. Truly I tell you, if you have faith as small as a mustard seed, you can say to this mountain, move from here to there, and it will move. Nothing will be impossible for you."[21]

So, then what is hard to do, to say, "I am righteous by faith in Jesus Christ," or to perform Sabbath observation? Or how do you know you are a child of God with your

---

[18] 1 John 1:9
[19] Hebrews 10:2
[20] Romans 14:23
[21] Matthew 17:20

name written in the Lamb's Book of Life?
Simply by faith. There is no other proof
required except to believe. Under Grace,
you believe it and you possess it.

In Summary

You are not defined by what you do or fail
to do. Rather, you are a product of faith and
truth. Law burdened those who were under
it and robbed them of a free relationship
with God. Under the legal dispensation, law
itself was their master hooking them to
rules and guidelines.

But under Grace, we are set free in
order to fully enjoy God as our Father. We
have everything, not because we deserve
them, or we worked hard for them, but
because we did nothing, except to believe.

> Oh, the dimensions of grace
> divine,
> How easy, effortless – all is fine;
> But faulty, evilly, we were under
> law,
> Now through faith, we've no flaw

1 | LAW

Varieties of Laws: Law of Men

Humans are social beings. Humans are spiritual beings. They also have a body and a soul. This complex fusion of soul and matter exhibits various responses to different stimuli. In short, humans behave in a certain way. This behavior may not always be according to socially or spiritually-accepted norms. To channel the human energy in order to behave well or in an acceptable manner, law is used. Law, therefore, is, and has been, one of the primary instruments both God and humans use to manage human behavior.

Law can similarly be defined as rules that govern behavior. In essence, law is simply rules or principles. The combination of rule and principles informs that law is structured, dynamic, and predictable. Law may also be eternal in the sense that it perpetuates good behavior from one generation to another.

Although at the center of every law is the government of behavior, law itself manifests in different forms. Law can be legal, moral, canonical, customary, or ceremonial (as opposed to the *Decalogue*). Law can exist in nature, and physical bodies also respond to certain laws, such as the gravitational force. There are also other spiritual laws to which Paul refers to as, "…the law of my mind and…the law of sin that dwells within me."[22]

The law most common among humans is the legal or judicial law. This type of law may be defined as a set of rules passed by a legislature (or a Parliament) and which binds people to do or not to do certain things, and failure to do or not do may lead to certain defined sanctions or penalties. Laws passed by a legislature are known as statutes (or "Acts" of Parliament, usually shortened to *Acts*). This type of law is enforceable through the courts of law. It is enacted either through an authoritative, democratic body of elected officials, or it might be judge-made, in which case it is called caselaw or precedent.

Law can be framed from the region it emanated from or from its legal tradition. For example, law that began in England under the Viking Conqueror of England from Normandy, William the Conqueror, in 1066, is called common-law, and is passed from one generation to the next under a legal doctrine of *stare decisis*[23] in judicial decisions referred to above as precedents.

Law that has its genesis in Romeo-Justinian-French tradition is called *civil law*.

---

[22] See Romans 7:22-23, *infra*.
[23] Meaning, in Latin, "To stand by decided cases."

This type of law is found in books compiled for the purposes of adjudication, and these books or *codes* are collectively known as civil codes.

Law is extensive, and can be substantive or procedural, public or private, codified or unwritten, administrative or constitutional, criminal or civil,[24] contractual or tortuous, and so on. The common denominator between the divisions of laws mentioned above is that they are made by human beings. They are laws of men (of the humans).

This book is not concerned with legal law *per se*. The book makes reference to legal rules as a way of driving the conversation and illustrating similarities and trends.

Varieties of Laws: Law of God

Below we discuss in brevity moral law. The idea of morality is at the center of general ethics and rational morality, the science of rights and wrongs. Morality is

---

[24] Under the Common-Law legal system, the term "civil" has two meanings: It can mean a system (such as when it is opposed to Common-Law system) or it can be a private civil law as opposed to public criminal law. The State sues an individual under criminal law, while individuals or corporations sue each other under civil law. Criminal law's remedy is punishment, such as through fines or imprisonment; civil law's remedy is monetary compensation.

that area of higher law believed to have its source in God. Thus, Moral Law is a system.[25] It is a system of guidelines for moral behavior.

Generally, Moral Law is any division of good-behavior-law that places credence on religious good behavior. It is, however, important to note that it may not always exist within a religion or religious framework. Moral Law may be a part of an institution, family, club or fraternity. It is decreed through a set of guidelines, rules or *codes*. Moral Law, like law in general, may be written or unwritten. It may be legally enforceable through the courts or enforcement can be done through ecclesiastical bodies or agencies.

Certain words may be associated with Moral Law, the following Bible verses will illustrate:

> 89 Your **word**, Lord, is eternal;
>   it stands firm in the Heavens.
> 90 Your faithfulness continues through all generations; you established the earth, and it endures.
> 91 Your **laws** endure to this day,
>   for all things serve you.
> 92 If your **law** had not been my delight,
>   I would have perished in my affliction.

---

[25] Moral Law, Common-Law and Civil Law are systems; the first comes from God, the second from England and the third from France or Rome. The first is the law of God; the last two are laws of men.

LAW & GRACE

93 I will never forget your **precepts**,
for by them you have preserved my life.
94 Save me, for I am yours;
 I have sought out your **precepts**.
95 The wicked are waiting to destroy me, but I will ponder your **statutes**.
96 To all perfection I see a limit,
 but your **commands** are boundless.
97 Oh, how I love your **law**!
 I meditate on it all day long.
98 Your **commands** are always with me
 and make me wiser than my enemies.
99 I have more insight than all my teachers, for I meditate on your **statutes**.
100 I have more understanding than the elders, for I obey your precepts.
101 I have kept my feet from every evil path so that I might obey your **word**.
102 I have not departed from your **laws**,
 for you yourself have taught me.
103 How sweet are your **words** to my taste, sweeter than honey to my mouth!
104 I gain understanding from your **precepts**; therefore I hate every wrong path.
105 Your **word** is a lamp for my feet,
 a light on my path.
106 I have taken an oath and confirmed it, that I will follow your righteous **laws**.
107 I have suffered much; preserve my life, Lord, according to your **word**.
108 Accept, Lord, the willing praise of my mouth, and teach me your **laws**.
109 Though I constantly take my life in my hands, I will not forget your **law**.
110 The wicked have set a snare for me,
 but I have not strayed from your

precepts.

111 Your **statutes** are my heritage forever; they are the joy of my heart.

112 My heart is set on keeping your **decrees** to the very end.

113 I hate double-minded people,
   but I love your **law**.

114 You are my refuge and my shield;
   I have put my hope in your **word**.

115 Away from me, you evildoers,
   that I may keep the **commands** of my God!

116 Sustain me, my God, according to your **promise**, and I will live;
   do not let my hopes be dashed.

117 Uphold me, and I will be delivered;
   I will always have regard for your decrees.

118 You reject all who stray from your **decrees**, for their delusions come to nothing.

119 All the wicked of the earth you discard like dross; therefore I love your **statutes**.

120 My flesh trembles in fear of you;
   I stand in awe of your **laws**.[26]

The next Bible verses are like the first:

7 The **law** of the Lord is perfect, converting the soul:
the **testimony** of the Lord is sure, making wise the simple.
8 The **statutes** of the Lord are right,

---

[26] Psalm 119: 89-120 (emphasis added)

rejoicing the heart:
the **commandment** of the Lord is pure,
enlightening the eyes.
9 The **fear of the Lord** is clean, enduring
forever: the judgments of the Lord are
true and righteous altogether.
10 They are more precious than gold,
> than much pure gold;
> they are sweeter than honey,
> > than honey from the honeycomb.
> 11 By them your servant is warned;
> > in keeping them there is great
reward.
> 12 But who can discern their own
errors?
> > Forgive my hidden faults.
> 13 Keep your servant also from willful
sins;
> > may they not rule over me.
> > Then I will be blameless,
> > > innocent of great transgression.
14 May these words of my mouth and this meditation
> of my heart
> > be pleasing in your sight,
> > Lord, my Rock and my Redeemer.[27]

The following words (taken from the two verses above) usually represent Moral Law: Law, laws, precepts, commands, judgments, decrees, testimony, commandments, words, word, promise, and fear of God. The Bible may sometimes use them interchangeably, and other times to denote certain actions or

---

[27] Psalm 19: 1-14 (Emphasis added)

duties. They all involve an exercise in morality. At the end of each moral pronouncement is a Supreme Being or God.

Although this book is tailored towards Christianity, Moral Law is not a quintessence of Christianity. Moral Law is the law of the entire world, and is applicable to Muslims, Christians, Buddhists, Hindus or any other unrecognized religion. God and the right way to approach Him is the theme and agenda of Moral Law.

There are three (3) branches of Moral Law. These are Canon Law, Divine Law, and the Mosaic Law (the Mosaic Law is further divided into two categories, and these are: Ceremonial Law and the *Decalogue* or Ten Commandments.

The first branch of Moral Law is Canon Law. It is Christian law or church or ecclesiastical law. It comprises ordinances,[28] decrees, edicts and regulations pronounced by a body with ecclesiastical authority. Canon Law, for example, governs the Catholic Church. But Canon Law may be enacted for any other Christian organization which is binding upon its adherents or members. Evangelicals, Pentecostals, Charismatics, the Anglican Church (the

---

[28] In Common-law, ordinances are special type of legislated pronouncements or acts of parliament that may be made by bodies with legislative powers, such as a National or Legislative Assembly. They are special types of statutes.

Church of England) may be regulated by sets of ordinances and regulations binding upon their members.

The second branch of Moral Law is Divine Law. It is the body of law that is considered to have been given, directly or indirectly, by God or gods. In Christianity, Divine Law is Moral Law given by God to His people through specially appointed (or anointed) personalities, such as Moses and Jesus. By its nature, Divine Law comes from a divine, transcendental source. It is imbued in the will (or enablement) of God or gods. It is God-made law.

The third branch of Moral Law is the Mosaic Law. As the name implies, this was the law God gave to the children of Israel through Moses in the Old Testament. It is divided into the *Decalogue* and the ceremonial law.

The Ten Commandments are a set of ten dos and don'ts God gave to the people through Moses. These ten *commandments* are reproduced below:

> **20** And God spoke all these words:
> 2 "I am the Lord your God, who brought you out of Egypt, out of the land of slavery.
> 3 [**1**] "You shall have no other gods before me.
> 4 [**2**] "You shall not make for yourself an image in the form of anything in Heaven above or on

the earth beneath or in the waters below.
5 You shall not bow down to them or worship them; for I, the Lord your God, am a jealous God, punishing the children for the sin of the parents to the third and fourth generation of those who hate me,
6 but showing love to a thousand generations of those who love me and keep my commandments.
7 [**3**] "You shall not misuse the name of the Lord your God, for the Lord will not hold anyone guiltless who misuses his name.
8 [**4**] "Remember the Sabbath day by keeping it holy.
9 Six days you shall labor and do all your work,
10 but the seventh day is a sabbath to the Lord your God. On it you shall not do any work, neither you, nor your son or daughter, nor your male or female servant, nor your animals, nor any foreigner residing in your towns.
11 For in six days the Lord made the Heaven and the earth, the sea, and all that is in them, but he rested on the seventh day. Therefore the Lord blessed the Sabbath day and made it holy.
12[**5**] "Honor your father and your mother, so that you may live long in the land the Lord your God is giving you.

13[**6**] "You shall not murder.
14[**7**] "You shall not commit adultery.
15[**8**] "You shall not steal.
16[**9**] "You shall not give false testimony against your neighbor.
17[**10**] "You shall not covet your neighbor's house. You shall not covet your neighbor's wife, or his male or female servant, his ox or donkey, or anything that belongs to your neighbor."[29]

These commands are consisting in ten statements or commandments. The *Decalogue* prescribe neither an enforcement mechanism nor do they offer remedies, except for the fifth commandment: "Honor thy father and thy mother, *that thy days may be long upon the land which the Lord thy God giveth thee.*"[30] The assumption is that these commands were to be obeyed without any promise of rewards or sanctions. They originated from the Supreme Being and compliance to them was total. The *Decalogue* demanded full submission.

Inherent in the *Decalogue* was the idea that they were given to people who were expected to know what they were obeying. The children of Israel should have been home-schooled in the intricacies of a historical deity who had redeemed them.

---

[29] Exodus 20:1-17
[30] *Ibid.*, verse 12, KJV (emphasis added)

God gave the law in a matter-of-factly-way – assuming that the people already knew Him and were expected to obey Him.

It could be argued, that most of these commandments were the foundation of the modern criminal law, codified in most nations' penal or criminal codes. The *Codex Hammurabi*, for example, borrowed a great deal from these commandments and from the judicial precepts.[31] The only difference is that modern criminal law comes with benefits and sanctions, and an imbedded procedural enforcement mechanism. The Ten Commandments were mostly prescriptive,[32] and not proscriptive.[33] Violating them attracted divine punishment, but this was only in the minds of the recipients of the law; the law itself had no stated sanctions for its violation.

However, all the sanctions, rewards or punishments, dubbed "blessings and curses"[34] not specifically stated in the *Decalogue*, were contained in the Ceremonial Law (also known as Ceremonial Precepts).

Ceremonial Law consists of rules, observations, and guidelines on various religious matters. God gave these to Moses through the Torah[35] or the Law of Moses, or the first five books of the Old

---

[31] See footnote 41, *infra*.
[32] Or rigid
[33] Or liberal
[34] See Deuteronomy 28
[35] Also known as Chameesha Choomshey Torah

Testament. These books are *Bresheit* (Genesis), *Shemot* (Exodus), *Vayicra* (Leviticus), *Bamidbar* (Numbers), and *Devarim* (Deuteronomy).[36] *My Jewish Learning* (MJL) describes the Torah in this fashion:

> The Torah (Hebrew for "the teachings") is the name given to the Five Books of Moses which come at the very beginning of the Bible. These books form the basis of all Jewish law and practice. A Torah scroll is a parchment scroll on which all five books have been inscribed by a specially trained calligrapher. Torah scrolls are typically kept in synagogues, in a special cabinet called an ark. On Mondays, Thursdays, and Saturdays the Torah scroll is removed from the ark, paraded around the room, and then a portion of the Torah is chanted aloud for the whole community. In Judaism, Torah scrolls are considered the holiest objects and are handled with extreme affection and care. In Judaism, these books are called the Torah, or "the Law." The Law of Moses, also called the Mosaic Law, primarily refers to

---

[36] BBC, "The Torah," < https://www.bbc.co.uk/religion/religions/judaism/texts/torah.shtml#:~:text=It%20is%20the%20central%20and,%2C%20and%20Devarim%20(Deuteronomy)> retrieved on November 23rd, 2020

> the Torah or the first five books
> of the Hebrew Bible. Traditionally
> believed to have been written by
> Moses, most academics now
> believe they had many authors.[37]

Generally, Ceremonial Law deals with acceptable forms of tabernacle worship,[38] cleansing rituals[39] and judicial precepts.[40] These laws were transient; they were specific to the Jewish nation and to Judaism. As alluded to earlier, *Codex Hammurabi*[41] borrowed heavily from them.

The oft-quoted, "Eye for an Eye," Leviticus injunction, thus, "And a man who injures his countryman – as he has done, so it shall be done to him [namely], fracture under/for fracture, eye under/for eye, tooth under/for tooth. Just as another person has received injury from him, so it will be given to him,"[42] features most notably in *Codex Hammurabi*, thus, "If a man destroy the eye of another man, they shall

---

[37] MJL, "What is the Torah?" < https://www.myjewishlearning.com/article/what-is-the-torah/> retrieved on November 23rd, 2020
[38] See Exodus 25–31 and 35–40
[39] See Leviticus 13 - 16
[40] See Exodus 21 and Deuteronomy 4
[41] A Babylonian code of law of ancient Mesopotamia, dated about 1754 BC. It was sanctioned by King Hammurabi. He was the sixth king of the First Babylonian dynasty of the Amorite tribe. He is believed to have reigned from c. 1792 BC to c. 1750 BC. The code outlived him.
[42] Lev. 24:19–21

destroy his eye. If one break a man's bone, they shall break his bone. If one destroy the eye of a freeman or break the bone of a freeman he shall pay one gold *mina*. If one destroy the eye of a man's slave or break a bone of a man's slave he shall pay one-half his price."[43] It can be argued that what has become of our civil society and its legal tradition was derived, chiefly, from Moral Law.

The Significance of Law

Without law, humanity could devolve into ungovernable confusion of anarchy. In a spiritual sense, law does the following:

1. It describes sin (or offense) – "What shall we say then? Is the law sin? God forbid. Nay, I had not known sin, but by the law: for I had not known lust, except the law had said, Thou shalt not covet."[44]

2. It arouses sin – "But sin, seizing its opportunity [chance] through the commandment, produced in me every kind of covetous desire. For apart from the law, sin is dead. Once I was alive apart from the law; but when the commandment came,

---

[43] *Codex Hammurabi*, Ex. Law #196
[44] Romans 7:7

sin sprang to life and I died. So, I discovered that the very commandment that was meant to bring life actually brought death. For sin, seizing its opportunity through the commandment, deceived me and through the commandment put me to death."[45]

3. It reveals sin – "Did that which is good, then, become death to me? Certainly not! But in order that sin might be exposed as sin, it produced death in me through what was good, so that through the commandment sin might become utterly sinful. We know that the law is spiritual; but I am unspiritual, sold as a slave to sin."[46]

   "For in my inner being I delight in God's law. But I see another law at work in my body, warring against the law of my mind and holding me captive to the law of sin that dwells within me."[47]

4. The law was the schoolmaster – "Wherefore the law was our schoolmaster to bring us unto

---

[45] Romans 7:8 – 11
[46] Romans 7:13 – 14
[47] Romans 7:22-23

Christ, that we might be justified by faith."[48]

"Let me put it another way. The law was our guardian until Christ came; it protected us until we could be made right with God through faith."[49]

5. Christ is end of the law and the beginning of Grace – "For Christ is the end of the law for righteousness to everyone that believeth."[50]

In Summary

Law dictates rules; Grace, by definition, is absence of rules. By keeping all rules under law, one evolves into a submissive, obedient and inoffensive human citizen. Grace needs no law (except love) to be approved. Under Grace, you do literally nothing to deserve approval. Law rewards compliance; Grace awards favors for doing nothing. Law is burdensome; Grace bequeaths no burden, except the burden not to carry any burdens. Law demands sinless perfection; Grace's only demand is that you *believe* you are perfect, irrespective

---

[48] Galatians 3:24, KJV (emphasis added)
[49] Galatians 3:24, NLT
[50] Romans 10:4

of your present spiritual circumstance. So, those who live by law must of necessity also be slaves of the law – doing all its bidding without question. But those who live by Grace are free, and free they are, indeed.

The framework under which law is discussed in this book is the *Decalogue* and various ceremonial laws in the Old Testament. In the ensuring chapters, the word "Law" may be used to encompass all the rules, words, word, decrees, regulations, commandments, precepts, statutes, orders, or judgments which formed the legal regime under the Old Testament. The word "law" is used in a general sense in this book. Similarly, the word "Grace" is used to denote the new era under Grace; the word "grace" may be used in a general sense to mean beauty, favor, and similarly-situated terms. And the word "Church" is used in the sense of the universal Body of Christ, and "church" may be used to refer to local Christian congregations.

> O grace, how amazing
> My heart awakes, up gazing
> O grace, what God has done
> Compares to anything but none.

2 | GRACE

Meaning of Grace

A toddler defined Grace as being "nice and gentle."[51] The concept of Grace (*chen* in Hebrew, *charis* in Greek) is based on the idea that God has chosen to accept us regardless of who we are. We do not need to do anything or please God in any way, except by believing in God's Grace. God has simply decided to accept us and adopt us as His own children. God has justified us - declaring us righteous and granting us eternal life without any merit on our part.[52]

God is reconciling us to Himself, not counting our sins against us, even when we have violated the Law.[53] In reconciling us to Himself, God takes care of our past sins which we have confessed, repented of and turned away from.[54] In Grace, God tells us that we are as if we have not sinned. Grace provides us with the means to be righteous without doing one single act of righteousness. It does not depend on us (except, in believing in the finished work of

---

[51] Cuteravive Mwewa, during a conversation with her Dad, Monday, November 23rd, 2020
[52] See 2 Corinthians 5:21 and Romans 3:21-22
[53] 2 Corinthians 5:19
[54] Psalm 32:5; Proverbs 28:13; 1 John 1:9

Christ).

Grace grows as sin increases. The more sinful, the more wicked and the more we have offended God, the more Grace abounds. Apostle Paul asks: "Shall we continue in sin, that grace may abound?"[55] In principle, yes. The more we sin, the more Grace abounds. However, practically, it defeats the premise on which we were forgiven. As will be argued in this book, even if we want to continue in sin, Grace makes it difficult to do so. A person who has received Grace and is saved through faith in Christ Jesus, may not sin even if they want to because a new nature has formed in them:

> Grace and peace be multiplied to you through the knowledge of God and of Jesus our Lord. His divine power has given us everything we need for life and godliness through the knowledge of Him who called us by His own glory and excellence. Through these He has given us His precious and magnificent promises, so that through them you may become partakers of the *divine nature*, now that you have escaped the corruption in the world caused by evil desires[56]

---

[55] Romans 6:1
[56] 2 Peter 1:3-4, (emphasis added)

We are partakers of a new nature, a divine nature, by Grace through faith. This Grace grows in us as we know God and our Lord Jesus Christ more and more: "Grace…be multiplied to you through the knowledge of God and of Jesus our Lord."[57] Grace is who God and our Lord Jesus Christ are; the more we know them, the more in Grace we grow.

Grace is the central message of the New Testament. It effuses in all the doctrinal particles of the Bible. It must inform character, substance, process and procedures of the New Testament. It is the central theme and the overarching program of the Gospel message. Without Grace, we are still stuck in the old regime and are still under its curse. Grace has freed us from the power of sin and created in us a new nature in Christ. Indeed:

> The concept of Grace is most prominently found in the New Testament in the epistles of Paul. The standard greeting in the Greek ancient world generally involved the verb *charein*. Paul's greeting, however, was unique, combining the Hebrew greeting, shalom [(*eirene* in Greek) with the word *charis* [cavri]. This in itself is enough to note that Paul is thinking and not simply reacting as

---

[57] 2 Peter 1:2

he writes his greeting."[58]

All the major New Testament writers have also made Grace the center piece of their Gospels.[59] Every New Testament believer has received a measure of Christ's Grace: "To each one of us grace has been given as Christ apportioned it."[60]

Salvation: Grace and Faith

In his letter to the Ephesians, Paul writes, "For it is by grace you have been saved, through faith – and is not from yourselves, it is the gift of God."[61] "For it is by grace that you have been saved," is a revolutionary statement. Hitherto, no-one was righteous apart from the Law. To be accepted before God, one had to do all the requirements of the Law. Law itself was diverse. It included natural law, Mosaic Law, the *Decalogue*, and various ceremonial laws, rules and regulations given by God from generation to generation. Most prominent of these were to do with tabernacle worship and sacrifices.

The people who did all the requirements of the Law were righteous, at that time, by

---

[58] https://www.biblestudytools.com/dictionary/grace/
[59] See John 1:16-17; Matt 20:1-16; or Luke 14:16-24
[60] Ephesians 4:7
[61] Ephesians 2:8

that standard. The problem was, no-one could do all the requirements of the Law. People fell short.

There was no human being capable of obeying all the countless number of rules. A new way of fulfilling God's righteousness was needed. Amazingly enough it came, and not as men expected. It had nothing to do with Law at all – it had everything to do without Law. Therefore, "For the law was given through Moses; grace and truth came through Jesus Christ."[62] It was Grace, and it came by Jesus Christ.

But this was not a surprise. A long time ago God had done something that gave an idea what he would do in the future. He had declared Abram righteous simply by Abram putting his faith in God. Abram was considered righteous apart from the Law: "Abram believed the LORD, and he credited it to him as righteousness."[63] In other words, Abram simply believed the LORD. And the LORD simply counted him as righteous because of his faith. Righteousness was, thus, achieved without the instrument of the Law. This changed everything.

It means, in essence, that you do not have to do anything, say anything to please God or sacrifice anything to be accepted by God. All God will be pleased with is you

---

[62] John 1:17
[63] Genesis 15:6

trusting His Son or Him, "And without faith it is impossible to please God."[64] In short, when you put your faith in Christ only, you have pleased God (as if you have done all the requirements of the Law) without doing any works. That is what is meant by "And if by grace, then it cannot be based on works; if it were, grace would no longer be grace."[65] Right there, Grace means no works; no works means not doing anything, only believing. Law means doing something or prohibition from doing something.

You can be filthy, dirty, evil or whatever exemplifies wrongfulness, but when you put your trust in Christ (you believe), you are transformed into righteousness. This is for everyone – not only Christians and Jews, for everyone. This also means that no-one can determine when you are saved – most people you may think are not saved, can be saved within a blink of an eye – by doing nothing at all, simply believing. This is a hard message for those who believe, implicitly or explicitly, that someone must do something to be, for example, saved. Nothing. Zero. All they need is faith in Christ, and they are righteous.

This also means that more people, *per capita*, may be going to Heaven than Hell. Why? Because salvation, for example, can

---

[64] Hebrews 11:6
[65] Romans 11:6

come in the blink of an eye before one passes from this life to the next. Simply by believing in Christ!

You are no more righteous at the point of salvation than when you "do" God's will or "serve" God. You do not increase your righteousness by serving in the Kingdom of God. You do not increase your righteousness by giving more. You do not increase your righteousness by praying more. You do not increase your righteousness by being committed more, or doing more for God. You are simply righteous by Grace through faith in Christ. All other teachings are human efforts to try and make you keep their laws and traditions. Grace saves you, truth sets you free.

In Summary

Salvation through Law was not possible because no-one kept the Law. Moses' laws were good and righteous:

> For sin, seizing its opportunity through the commandment, deceived me and through the commandment put me to death. So then, the law is holy, and the commandment is holy, righteous, and good. Did that which is good, then, become death to me? Certainly not! But in order that sin

> might be exposed as sin, it
> produced death in me through
> what was good, so that through
> the commandment sin might
> become utterly sinful.[66]

But Law could not save a soul. Law introduced sin, and sin led to death. Without the Law, there could be no sin because sin is the transgression of the Law: "Whosoever committeth sin transgresseth also the law: for sin is the transgression of the law."[67] Righteousness is achieved purely by Grace through faith in Jesus Christ. No works are required. No human effort or sacrifice is needed, only faith.

> Oh, the mounds and piles of His grace
> Anyone, everyone has in it a place
> Oh, the simplicity of this faith divine
> To hear Him say, "You're mine."

---

[66] Romans 7:11-13, NIV
[67] 1 John 3:4, NKV

3 | THREE UNCHANGING TRUTHS

Sin, Conscience and Salvation

There are three unchanging truths of Grace, and this is what sets Grace apart from Law: Those who are saved cannot continue to sin; conscience is the soul's umpire; and true salvation is never lost.

Salvation Neutralizes Sin's Power

Those who are saved cannot continue to sin: "No one who is born of God will continue to sin, because God's seed remains in them; they cannot go on sinning, because they have been born of God."[68] This verse does not say, "They are unable to sin," it does say that they have no will to sin.

If you are saved, you will find it very shameful, hard and even uncomfortable when you sin. In other words, you do not enjoy sin anymore, even when you think you will enjoy it. The unsaved, however, do enjoy their sins. Because in a saved person, there is no longer the willingness to sin. In many cases, even when they temporarily go

---

[68] 1 John 3:9, NIV

away from Christ, they will come back.

And this leads to the next verse: "They went out from us, but they didn't belong to us; for if they had belonged to us, they would have continued with us. But they left, that they might be revealed that none of them belong to us."[69] The assumption here is that, if someone claims that they were saved and then they did backslid, they were not saved in the first place. That is true in tandem with the spirit of Grace. If you want to prove this wrong, try to live a sinful life, and if you're truly saved, you will fail, you will give up. For the regenerate, there is only one way of living happily, a life of freedom and goodness, and that is by not desiring sin. Not because they want to, but because they are. They are now a new creature,[70] in the strictest sense of this phrase, and their nature has been internally altered. Because whom the Son sets free, is free, indeed.

The rationale is germane here. Grace says, "Do everything. Say everything. Be everything." Law says just the opposite. But the difference is that, while Law prohibits you from doing, saying or being evil, it is powerless to prevent you from sinning. Grace, however, tells you to do everything, say everything and be everything, and still you cannot volitionally sin. Law is bondage;

---

[69] 1 John 2:19
[70] 2 Corinthians 5:17

Grace is liberty. As it is written, "For sin shall no longer be your master, because you are not under the law, but under grace."[71]

But here is a caveat. Grace is planted like a seed in you. It grows as you grow in the knowledge of God and of Christ. If you stop growing in the knowledge of God, you may stagnate Grace in your own life.

The Umpire of Conscience

As stated earlier, that there were three unchanging truths of Grace. First, we discussed the truth that those who are saved cannot continue to sin. Second, we discuss the truth that our conscience is our umpire/referee: "And by this we will know that we belong to the truth, and will assure our hearts in His presence: If our hearts condemn us, God is greater than our hearts, and He knows all things. Beloved, if our hearts do not condemn us, we have confidence before God…"[72] At regeneration, something special happens: "I will put my law in their minds and write it on their hearts. I will be their God, and they will be my people."[73] This was a promise of Grace. When the Law was given, it was written on tablets and put in the temple. But God changed all that and now He

---

[71] Romans 6:14
[72] 1 John 3:19-21, NIV
[73] Jeremiah 31:33

writes it on our hearts and puts it in our minds. The temple is now ourselves, and the Holy of Holies is in our hearts.

Remember that all that Moses did was to give the Law. The Law introduced sin, because sin is "the transgression of the law."[74] To transgress the Law is to break or violate or disobey it. This is a double-impact statement. It means that Law effectively creates sin; and also, that sin itself means the violation of the Law, and this is what it means: "Everyone who sins is breaking God's law, for all sin is contrary to the law of God."[75]

In other words, if there is no Law, there is no sin because there is nothing to violate. If God did not say, "…you must not eat from the tree of the knowledge of good and evil, for when you eat from it you will certainly die,"[76] if Adam had eaten from it without this command, they would not have sinned. They only sinned, not because they ate, but by eating from the tree they violated God's command not to eat. Similarly, if there is no *Decalogue* or the Ten Commandments stating that you shall not kill, steal or covet another person's partner, even if you killed, stole or coveted, you would not be sinning because there would be no rule, command or law to break.

Therefore, when God gave the

---

[74] 1 John 3:4b
[75] 1 John 3:4
[76] Genesis 2:17

command in the Garden of Eden, He also put the potential for people to sin if they made a wrong choice. When Moses introduced the Law, he also with it introduced the possibility, and strength, of sin. But that is the essence of free will, that humans can choose good and evil by themselves.

When God introduced the Law, He had also at the same time reserved Grace – immediately man and woman sinned, or violated God's command, God provided a plan for their redemption. But it is Christ who came with Grace and truth: "For the law was given through Moses; grace and truth came through Jesus Christ."[77]

Law is now written on our hearts and stored in our minds. When we violate it, there is internally a referee which blows the whistle. It is called conscience. When we get saved, our conscience becomes alive, and it tells us when we have violated God's internal law (the greatest of which is a command to love God and others). If we violate it, we are without peace, we are troubled until we confess and do as it says. When we get saved, truth comes to live at the center of our hearts – we begin to know the truth. We do not need another person to tell us the truth; we will know it. Others may only confirm it, but we will know the truth.

---

[77] John 1:17

The knowledge of the Truth (Jesus Christ) is a gracious proposition. If truth was found somewhere in some temple in the box, you would excuse your sins because you would claim that you had no access to the Law. With the truth resident in our heart, that excuse is eliminated. But with truth also residing in us, our standard of holiness is very high – because every word, action, motive or attitude is weighed in time.

It means, humanly speaking, that this new arrangement will make it hard to be without peace as we will constantly be reminded of our short-comings. And there is good news, Grace. Truth in our own hearts is tempered with Grace. Both truth and Grace came by Christ. Grace is like a bucket of water that extinguishes the fire of sin. The more Grace you pour on sin, the easily extinguished sin becomes.

Law is closer to us than before, but Grace is even closer. The more laws there are, the more sin in the world there will be. Moreover, the more sin there is, the more Grace increases: "The law was brought in so that the trespass might increase. But where sin increased, grace increased all the more."[78] It does not, therefore, matter the level of sin in the world. If there is less sin, there is less Grace. But if sin increases, so does Grace. The things we call "big" sins, in

---

[78] Romans 5:20

fact, have more Grace than the "small" ones. The person who has cheated, committed adultery, murdered and committed treason receives more Grace from God than one who barely forgot to say sorry. The parts of the world with more sins have more Grace available to them than those parts with less sins. So, there is no winning for sin and Satan. This is what defeats Satan's plans. The thinking that the "biggest" sinners among us go to Hell, may be reasonable but not biblical. What goes to Hell is failure to accept Grace (failure to believe in Christ), not the quantity, quality or intensity of the sin.

Therefore, here is how the four interact, Law and sin, on one hand; and truth and Grace, on the other: Law introduces sin, but it is another way to introduce truth as well. So, this should settle the question of why introduce the Law if it also introduces sin. We can affirm that the main product of Law is truth, and sin is its side-effect. But God has a cure for the sin side-effect; it is called Grace.

To the end, why discuss Grace and conscience? Grace basically means that everything has become lawful. But not every lawful thing is beneficial or can build you up: "All things are lawful, but not all things are profitable; all things are lawful, but not all edify."[79] Under Grace,

---

[79] 1 Corinthians 10:23

everything is essentially permitted, but it may not be beneficial to you or your fellow brothers and sisters. For example, eating food sacrificed to idols or drinking wine (not getting drunk) is permitted, but you may not eat it due to another's conscience: "If your brother is distressed by what you eat, you are no longer acting in love. Do not by your eating destroy your brother, for whom Christ died."[80] Another example, smoking may not be sin, but it might cause someone to be distressed, so you may not smoke in public for your brethren's conscience.

Spiritual orientation also matters. For Christians in Africa, for example, going to a cinema theater to watch a movie may be distressing to many, but the consciences of the North American Christians are fine with it. Therefore, if you are with a Christian brother from Africa, you may not enter a movie theater to protect his conscience, but you could enter with a Canadian brother.

But sometimes conscience must be tamed and trained. For example, most African Christians would not make friends with those who are homosexuals, but Americans might. In this scenario, conscience must be trained because this is an issue of love, not Law or truth: "If our hearts condemn us, God is greater than our

---

[80] Romans 14:15

hearts, and He knows all things."[81] In other words, when it comes to matters of love, God is greater than our consciences, "Whoever does not love does not know God, because God is love."[82] So, even if your conscience incites you to hate (because you feel like supporting a habit), you will ignore your conscience because the Greatest Commandment has overridden your conscience. Under Grace, a Christian has the ultimate freedom to do anything, say anything and acting in any way if his or her own conscience does not condemn them: "Beloved, if our hearts do not condemn us, we have confidence before God…"[83]

However, in matters of love, even if your conscience condemns you, ignore it and do the loving act or gesture. The Bible is clear, if you have no love, you do not know God, either. And Grace increases with an increase in the knowledge of God who is love.[84]

Moreover, Grace has given everyone an opinion on any issue. In other words, you can believe anything you want. But again, conscience is the referee; the thing or things you believe must be helpful to you and to your relationship with your God: "Keep your belief about such matters between

---

[81] 1 John 3:19-21
[82] 1 John 4:8
[83] 1 John 3:19-21
[84] 1 John 4:8, *supra*.

yourself and God. Blessed is the one who does not condemn himself by what he approves."[85] If your conscience does not condemn what you are thinking, eating, doing, planning or experiencing, then, as far as right and wrong is concerned, you are good. Literally, "Therefore, there is now no condemnation for those who are in Christ Jesus,"[86] who are under Grace.

True Salvation Is Never Lost

The third and last truth of Grace is that no-one whom the Father has accepted can lose their salvation. First, no matter the temptation, God will always provide a way of escape: "No temptation has overtaken you except what is common to mankind. And God is faithful; he will not let you be tempted beyond what you can bear. But when you are tempted, he will also provide a way out so that you can endure it."[87] Two things are clear in this verse. That temptations are common to all and they are inevitable, they will come. Temptations are triggered by several factors including our own desires and to some extent, the devil. This means that many people who believe will feel like quitting and getting on an easy way out. And, no matter the temptations,

---

[85] Romans 14:22
[86] Romans 8:1
[87] 1 Corinthians 10:13, NIV

God will make sure that you are able to endure it. This is only possible under Grace.

Second, God has two options for those who believe but continue to sin willfully.

In the first place, He will provide a strong rebuke: "…the Lord disciplines the one he loves, and he chastens everyone he accepts as his son."[88] God is Sovereign, so He can do anything to discipline His own. How and what He does to discipline His own, is His prerogative. But whomever it has been done to, will understand it and know that they are under God's strong hand of discipline. It also can be idiosyncratic, meaning that it differs from person to person. What is, however, clear is that one will know that they are under discipline.

In the second place, God will take them if they continue to sin willfully: "For anyone who eats and drinks without recognizing the body eats and drinks judgment on himself. That is why many among you are weak and sick, and a number of you have fallen asleep. Now if we judged ourselves properly, we would not come under judgment.…"[89] And:

> It is actually reported that there is sexual immorality among you, and of a kind that even pagans do not tolerate: A man is sleeping with his

---

[88] Hebrews 12:6
[89] 1 Corinthians 11:29-31, NIV

> father's wife. And you are proud. Shouldn't you rather have gone into mourning and have put out of your fellowship the man who has been doing this? For my part, even though I am not physically present, I am with you in spirit. As one who is present with you in this way, I have already passed judgment in the name of our Lord Jesus on the one who has been doing this. So, when you are assembled and I am with you in spirit, and the power of our Lord Jesus is present, *hand this man over to Satan for the destruction of the flesh, so that his spirit may be saved on the day of the Lord*.[90]

Satan can destroy the body, but God will spare the soul. Similarly, those whose work is not of faith, will still be saved but lose some rewards: "If it is burned up, the builder will suffer loss but yet will be saved – even though only as one escaping through the flames."[91]

Third, the works of the Holy Spirit in the world. The Holy Spirit has a dual role to play in the sinner's and the believer's lives. For the sinner (the world), the Holy Spirit brings or induces a feeling or repugnance for sin: "And when he comes, he will convict the world of its sin, and of God's

---

[90] 1 Corinthians 5:1-5, NIV (emphasis added)
[91] 1 Corinthians 3:15

righteousness, and of the coming judgment."[92] You must understand that under Grace, it is not the role of a human agent to pass judgment on another human being: "Judge not, that ye be not judged."[93] It is only the Holy Spirit who plays that role, "...he will convict the world of its sin, and of God's righteousness, and judgment."[94] And even the Holy Spirit does not condemn people, he merely convinces or convicts them so that they can repent. Notice also that judgment for the devil has already been passed; he was found guilty or condemned, "...and about judgment, because the prince of this world now stands condemned."[95] The devil cannot be redeemed; his fate has been sealed, "...into the eternal fire that has been prepared for the devil and his angels!"[96] God never prepared Hell for humans. Those who will go to Hell get there by choice – because they were not saved in the first place. Jesus said, "All that the Father giveth me shall come to me; and him that cometh to me I will in no wise cast out."[97]

Under Grace, the Holy Spirit helps believers to love and know more about Jesus so that they can continue to believe.

---

[92] John 16:8
[93] Matthew 7:1
[94] John 16:8
[95] John 16:11
[96] Matthew 25:41
[97] John 6:37

He also provides help against sin by the production of self-control: "…for God gave us a spirit not of fear but of power and love and self-control."[98] Therefore, there are more safeguards to the maintenance of Grace through faith than a believer can ask for.

Now there are two passages of Scripture that seem to challenge, directly or indirectly, the concept of Grace. We have established the three unchanging truths of Grace: That those who are saved cannot continue to sin; that our conscience is our umpire/referee; and that no-one whom the Father has accepted can lose their salvation. These truths about Grace only operate also based on another unchanging truth, that God has not silenced our wills through Grace. This is what makes human beings different from all other creatures – our will to choose, decide or reject. God has provided for complete forgiveness of all sins – past, present and future. But a person can choose not to accept it, although God has accepted them. Grace works seamlessly in those who are willing (to live a godly life, a life of love and humility, and so on). Those who are proud, high-minded and willfully disobedient will not fall from Grace, but will destroy themselves.

And let us briefly discuss the concept of "falling from grace." It is not used in the

---

[98] 2 Timothy 1:7

context of sin, but of Law. You cannot do anything that God cannot forgive. You cannot sin and get beyond Grace. Grace works mightily where there is sin, not in the absence of it. Grace checks on sin. But Grace is powerless with Law. The two are mutually exclusive – you can only have one and not the other. If you are under Grace and continue to follow the Law, you have strictly fallen from Grace: "Again I testify to every man who gets himself circumcised that he is obligated to obey the whole Law. You who are trying to be justified by the Law have been severed from Christ; you have fallen away from grace."[99]

Let us look at the first instance of passages that seem to challenge Grace: "Because of the multiplication of wickedness, the love of most will grow cold. But the one who perseveres to the end will be saved. And this gospel of the kingdom will be preached in all the world as a testimony to all nations, and then the end will come…"[100] Most people preach on this passage selectively but it must be considered in totality. There is both truth and Grace in this passage, and both came by Christ Jesus.[101]

Remember that in the examination of Grace and truth, both must balance each other. Grace without truth would give

---

[99] Galatians 5:3-4
[100] Matthew 24:13-14
[101] See John 1:17

license to humanity's basic instinct for pleasure. However, truth without Grace would make salvation almost impossible. Here is how truth and Grace balances each other. There is a multiplication of sins and wickedness in the world. This leads to coldness towards God. But there is also the preaching of the Gospel (Good News) which warms up the hearts of the world. As a result, the world will always be in a state of balance. When the Lord's prophet thought that he was the only one left, God educated him: "Lord, they have killed Your prophets and torn down Your altars. I am the only one left, and they are seeking my life as well"? And what was the divine reply to him? "I have reserved for Myself seven thousand men who have not bowed the knee to Baal."[102] Sin will increase and discourage many, but so will Grace through preaching and many will be saved.

The second passage is like the first:

> It is impossible for those who have once been enlightened, who have tasted the heavenly gift, who have shared in the Holy Spirit, who have tasted the goodness of the word of God and the powers of the coming age — and then have fallen away—to be restored again to repentance, because they themselves are crucifying the Son

---

[102] Romans 11:4

> of God all over again and
> subjecting Him to open
> shame....[103]

This passage is akin to one in Matthew, "Then goeth he, and taketh with himself seven other spirits more wicked than himself, and they enter in and dwell there: and the last state of that man is worse than the first. Even so shall it be also unto this wicked generation,"[104] alluding to a person from whom demons have been cast and who goes on sinning. The word "impossible" in Hebrews 6, applies to will – to the person who wills not to repent. God's Grace works by patience: "The Lord is not slow in keeping his promise, as some understand slowness. Instead he is patient with you, not wanting anyone to perish, but everyone to come to repentance."[105]

The surest sign that God's Grace is based on God's love (patience is the first part of the fruit of the Holy Spirit)[106] is in His patience towards those who have not yet decided to believe. If time is removed, the entire creation may look like it has been on a standstill. And God, who exists outside time, is patient enough to graciously afford humanity a chance to repent and mend their ways. That is Grace in operation.

---

[103] Hebrews 6:5-6
[104] Matthew 12:45
[105] 2 Peter 3:9, see also footnote 246
[106] See Galatians 5:22-23

There is one impossible thing even for God to do, He cannot trump over humanity's will, that is what makes humans like gods. But if any man repents and comes back to God, they will be accepted by God.

In Summary

Grace is not Law. It cannot be like Law. Under Law, salvation was limited. Under Grace, salvation is limitless and is permanent. External prerogatives rule under Law. In other words, it is only law because it is written down in codes or on paper. However, under Grace, the law is written in the heart. And it is the law of love.

> Wonderful grace, O grace
> My soul has found a place
> For law ran me to duress
> Sin made Heaven even less
> But through truth am free
> And by grace, God's for me.

4 | EIGHT PRINCIPLES OF GRACE

1. Love is Refined

Love is refined. Under Law, we labored hard to follow the commandments; under Grace we love: "Owe nothing to anyone-except for your obligation to love one another. If you love your neighbor, you will fulfill the requirements of God's law."[107] We now owe God and other people love. It is a debt we must pay every day. Those who love have transcended both Law and truth. There is no greater law, no ultimate truth than to love God and to love one another.

2. Work is Redefined

Work is redefined. Grace defines work or works as faith. Believing in Jesus is our new work, not performing ceremonies. This sounds too simplistic. Because it is. We do not have to work for God with sweat and hard labor. Our work for God is believing in Jesus, first and foremost, and all other labors are of love. Jesus answered, "The work of God is this: To believe in the one

---

[107] Romans 13:8

he has sent."[108] That is why everyone who is saved has a reward, because their belief in Christ is also considered working for God under Grace.

In earnest, the only work before God that will survive is the work of faith and love. So, "And whatever you do, whether in word or deed, do it all in the name of the Lord Jesus, giving thanks to God the Father through him,"[109] and "So whether you eat or drink or whatever you do, do it all for the glory of God."[110] To be God's work, what we do must glorify and please God, and nothing pleases God unless it is of faith.[111]

Under Grace, God works, not us. God works through us – because it is only Him who is good and always does good. God gives us inspiration, motivation, the joy and the will to do the things He wants us to do.[112] Therefore, we have no right to boast in whatever we do or "accomplish" for God. God did it. God did it through us. We were only vessels.

3. Boldness to Enter

We enter boldly into the presence of

---

[108] John 6:29
[109] Colossians 3:17
[110] 1 Corinthians 10:31
[111] Hebrews 11:6
[112] See Philippians 2:13

God: "Let us then approach God's throne of grace with confidence, so that we may receive mercy and find grace to help us in our time of need."[113] Here is a very powerful truth: God's throne is now a Throne of Grace, not of law or only of truth. When God insisted that only those who were morally pure enter into His presence, only a few could qualify. God has now made access to His throne one of pure Grace. We are all invited, no matter our conditions. And when we are in there, we receive more Grace and mercy. In other words, we need not be afraid to approach God, because He will not judge us, but He will have mercy on us. When we meet Him in His presence, He also gives us more Grace to do and accomplish anything or defeat that which is bothering us. This makes our new life a pleasure – where we cannot be rejected for our sins, but we receive mercy; and where if we are overwhelmed, God reaches out with His Grace in order to enable us to continue in victory.

4. Love before Commitment

God loved us before we loved Him: "We love him, because he first loved us."[114] There are two parallel interpretations of this

---

[113] Hebrews 4:16
[114] 1 John 4:19

verse. First, that God gave us the capacity to love Him. Second, it was not our initiative to love Him first, it was His. These two approaches do not mean much until you consider another Scripture: "But God demonstrates his own love for us in this: While we were still sinners, Christ died for us."[115] If we want to love someone, it is always a person who either loves us first or has shown great likeness for us, not the person we do not love or our enemy. God did an unimaginable thing: He loved a sinner, a person who was defiant against His will. If you can love a person who is bad to you, that is Grace. If you can love a person in that way, then it does not depend on what that person does or says, it depends on nothing. God does not love us because of anything – He loves us in spite of anything. There is nothing we can do, say or think to warrant His love. Similarly, there is no sin or wrong-doing that can make God not love us.

God is not against us. He is for us. He is not scaring us. He is welcoming us. He is not judging us. He is rewarding us. He is not mad with us. He is celebrating us. That is the message of Grace. Paul was not chatting a new path; he was simply following the path God had willed for him.

God loves you whether you sin or not. He loves you when you are obedient; He

---

[115] Romans 5:8

also loves you when you are disobedient. All you need is accept His free gift of salvation by Grace through faith, and at that point God will put in you a system that wills to do God's will and fulfill God's purposes: "...for it is God who works in you to will and to act in order to fulfill his good purpose."[116] Apostle Paul came to this realization: "Not as though I had already attained, either were already perfect: but I follow after, if that I may apprehend that *for which also I am apprehended of Christ Jesus*."[117]

Under Grace, God makes us will. This does not violate our wills; it empowers them. Under the Law, they struggled to find perfect will. Under Grace, we are helped to find God's perfect will. The Holy Spirit helps us to find and do God's will. He resides in us for that purpose, and to glorify God through us.

The two verses of Scripture above[118] are very revealing. They basically intimate that we play a very limited role in the fulfillment of God's will in our lives. Once we are available to God, He moves us, and enables us to do all of His will. This means that we cannot boast of any achievement, because it is not us who won; it is God who makes us will, and then supplies the Grace to accomplish anything we have thus far accomplished. A fool thinks they have done

---

[116] Philippians 2:13
[117] Philippians 3:12 (emphasis added)
[118] See Philippians 2:13 and 3:12

whatever they have. No, it is God who wills, not us. It is God who grants strength, not ourselves. It is God who makes the connections, opens the doors wild, creates perfect opportunities and places us in the right spot. It is God who wills – not our human genius, wisdom or power. So, it is not by mighty nor by power. It is of, and by, God. If you are rich, God enabled you to gain riches. If you are powerful, God enabled you to attain power. And so on.

The fool says in his heart, "There is no God,"[119] and another fool did say this:

> What shall I do? I have no place to store my crops. Then he said, 'This is what I'll do. I will tear down my barns and build bigger ones, and there I will store all my grain and my goods. And I'll say to myself, 'You have plenty of good things laid up for many years. Take life easy; eat, drink and be merry.' But God said to him, 'You fool! This very night your life will be demanded from you. Then who will get what you have prepared for yourself?' This is how it will be with anyone who stores up things for himself but is not rich towards God.[120]

---

[119] Psalm 14:1
[120] See particularly Luke 12:21

It is better to both be rich in this world's riches, and to be rich in faith towards God.

You see, it does not matter much who we are or what we have done. It is God who allows us to enjoy what we enjoy: "Command those who are rich in this present world not to be arrogant nor to put their hope in wealth, which is so uncertain, but to put their hope in God, who richly provides us with everything for our enjoyment."[121] All is due to nothing but pure Grace; no works, no law, nothing but Grace!

"He who did not spare his own Son, but gave him up for us all – how will he not also, along with him, graciously give us all things?"[122] Even human logic can get this: If you have already given your precious thing to an enemy, what can't you give to your friends, let alone your children? That is why nothing can separate us from God except ourselves. Even then, God shall will in us to repent and follow Him.

Indeed, God wills through and within us. Arguments can and are made that, this act usurps our free will. Not at all; it, rather, empowers our free will. It empowers our wills to do and think on those things which are true, noble, right, pure, lovely, admirable, grand, excellent or

---

[121] 1 Timothy 6:17
[122] Romans 8:32

praiseworthy.[123] When we surrender our wills to Jesus, He gives us back His perfect will. That is not being passive creatures; we are actively involved in this. We are part of Him. We are God's temples: "Do you not know that your bodies are temples of the Holy Spirit, who is in you, whom you have received from God? You are not your own."[124] The purpose of, first the tabernacle, and then the temple, was to be a place of worship, a place where God would dwell among His people. God now resides in us – we are the new temples, not made of stone, but made of flesh. We MUST do God's will because He and us are intertwined. Doing God's will connects us to Heaven : "…your will be done, on earth as it is in Heaven."[125] By doing what God wants, we seamlessly make earth exactly as Heaven is. And by extension, when we surrender to God, our existence ceases to be ours, we become one with God – Him residing in us and us residing in Christ. Therefore, when God works through and in us, it is as if we and God are doing the same thing. Our wills become one. That is what brings perfect satisfaction.

5. Lost But Found

---

[123] See Philippians 4:8
[124] 1 Corinthians 6:19
[125] Matthew 6:10b

The Parable of the Prodigal Son illustrates how Grace works by love: God welcomes us back without any merit on our part:

> Jesus continued: "There was a man who had two sons. The younger one said to his father, 'Father, give me my share of the estate.' So, he divided his property between them.
>
> "Not long after that, the younger son got together all he had, set off for a distant country and there squandered his wealth in wild living. After he had spent everything, there was a severe famine in that whole country, and he began to be in need. So he went and hired himself out to a citizen of that country, who sent him to his fields to feed pigs. He longed to fill his stomach with the pods that the pigs were eating, but no one gave him anything.
>
> "When he came to his senses, he said, 'How many of my father's hired servants have food to spare, and here I am starving to death! I will set out and go back to my father and say to him: Father, I have sinned against heaven and against you. I am no longer worthy to be called your son; make me like one of your hired servants.' So he got up and went to his father. "But while he was still a long way off, his father saw him and was filled with compassion for him;

he ran to his son, threw his arms around him and kissed him.

"The son said to him, 'Father, I have sinned against Heaven and against you. I am no longer worthy to be called your son.'

"But the father said to his servants, 'Quick! Bring the best robe and put it on him. Put a ring on his finger and sandals on his feet. Bring the fattened calf and kill it. Let's have a feast and celebrate. For this son of mine was dead and is alive again; he was lost and is found.' So they began to celebrate.

"Meanwhile, the older son was in the field. When he came near the house, he heard music and dancing. So he called one of the servants and asked him what was going on. 'Your brother has come,' he replied, 'and your father has killed the fattened calf because he has him back safe and sound.'

"The older brother became angry and refused to go in. So his father went out and pleaded with him. But he answered his father, 'Look! All these years I've been slaving for you and never disobeyed your orders. Yet you never gave me even a young goat so I could celebrate with my friends. But when this son of yours who has squandered your property with prostitutes comes home, you kill the fattened calf for him!'

"'My son,' the father said, 'you are

> always with me, and everything I have is yours. 32 But we had to celebrate and be glad, because this brother of yours was dead and is alive again; he was lost and is found.'"[126]

The younger son freely received all that he was legally entitled to under his father's estate. His elder brother did not. The younger son squandered everything he had and turned up a beggar or worse. His elder brother continued to enjoy the tenancy of his father's estate. By law, the younger son had ceased to have any stake in his father's inheritance. He could only have any title to it at his father's mercy. It did not depend on the younger son anymore; it depended on his father to exercise that discretion he had over the estate; to reintegrate the younger son into it or keep the requirement of the law and deny him, basically keeping things the way they were. The father exercised his unfettered discretion[127] and allowed the young son in.

Customary law set the requirements; the younger son had become untitled to the inheritance. Truth was that the son had wasted his inheritance in wild living and he was to face his new reality and either die in poverty or work hard for his own means. But the son decided to fall into the hands of

---

[126] Luke 15:11–32
[127] Discretion that is fully unrestricted and without constraints

his father – because his father loved him? No, because he figured it out that his father had mercy, i.e. "How many of my father's hired servants have food to spare, and here I am starving to death!" What he came to his senses for was in regards to his father's attitude towards workers. He was willing to become a servant under his father's care. Why? Because his father would treat him better than the hiring master, as a worker.

However, when he came back to his father, he received Grace. Here is how Grace operated:

1) It forgave him;
2) It cleaned him;
3) It celebrated his return;
4) It reinstituted him into sonship, thus, into the inheritance;
5) Going by his older brother's reaction, it doubled his inheritance by default; and
6) It gave him and treated him with love.

In other words, mercy protects us from what we deserve, but Grace gives us access to what we do not deserve, and doubles the proceeds.

Grace is powerful. Grace is not based on a relationship. Read this: "For God so loved the world that He gave…"[128] That is Grace,

---

[128] John 3:16

because God first loved and then He gave. In other words, there were no actions from the recipient that preceded God's love. The sinner did not have to do anything to deserve the love. The sinner received God's love without meriting it. But the sinner MUST decide to go back to the Father, just like the Prodigal Son had to decide first and go back to his father. Grace is always abundant; but the recipient of it must decide (exercise their own will), otherwise the sinner or the one in need will die without appropriating or using it. What preaching does is introduce people to the already available Grace. It points them in the direction to receiving Grace.

For the sinner, Grace is abundant for salvation. For the saint, Grace is also available for times of need. As explained elsewhere, both Grace and truth operate together and they check on each other. If there was only truth without Grace, perhaps no person would be saved. And if there was only Grace without truth, salvation would be cheap and our lives would be a sham. Moreover, it is truth in us which causes us not to continue in sin: "If we say that we have no sin, we deceive ourselves, and the truth is not in us."[129] It is the truth in us that alerts us to sin. A person without truth in them will not know they have sinned, even if they had committed murder. They would

---

[129] 1 John 1:8

justify it for their own twisted aggrandizement. But anyone who has truth in them will know when they have sinned and will confess: "If we confess our sins, he is faithful and just and will forgive us our sins and purify us from all unrighteousness."[130] This process, effectively, is what keeps us pure on a daily basis. It is not that we do not sin (because if we say so, we will make God a liar), it is because when we do sin, the truth in us alerts us to it and we confess it. And God, through His Grace, keeps forgiving us.

Therefore, Grace through truth, alerts us to sin, and empowers us to confess. Forgiveness of sins and reconciliation are both acts of Grace. However, forgiveness does not depend on the object of forgiveness; it depends on God.

Reconciliation depends on the object. Thus, God has forgiven us of our sins without any of our volition involved but requires us to actively be ministers of reconciliation:

> Therefore if anyone is in Christ, he is a new creation. The old has passed away. Behold, the new has come! All this is from God, who reconciled us to Himself through Christ and gave us the ministry of reconciliation: that

---

[130] 1 John 1:9

> God was reconciling the world to Himself in Christ, not counting men's trespasses against them. And He has committed to us the message of reconciliation. Therefore we are ambassadors for Christ, as though God were making His appeal through us. We implore you on behalf of Christ: Be reconciled to God. *God made Him who knew no sin to be sin on our behalf, so that in Him we might become the righteousness of God.*[131]

There again lies ultimate Grace; Christ knew no sin but was made sin for us so that we might become the righteousness of God. We did nothing, He did everything. We deserved worse, He gave us the best. We were sinners, but God made Jesus sin. We were undeserving of Heaven, but Jesus became a way to Heaven for us. The only thing remaining is for us to transmit this message to all, just as an ambassador does. We are on earth as emissaries from Heaven – to spread the Word of Grace.

Not only does truth in us keep us from sinning, but also faith does. For by faith we know that sin is powerless; we are positionally dead with Christ and risen to righteousness: "What shall we say, then? Shall we go on sinning so that grace may

---

[131] 2 Corinthians 5:17-21 (emphasis added)

increase? By no means! We are those who have died to sin; how can we live in it any longer?"[132]

First, if we go on sinning, it is true Grace will increase (because Scripture itself says so,[133] and so we will still maintain a positive relationship with God if we confess.)

But, second, the truth is that sin has been decapitated in our lives by Christ's death – so we are dead to sin. Sin is no longer our master, we are no longer its slaves.[134] This is double victory; we have received Grace for sin, and sin has no power over us through Christ. The only challenge is that we appropriate all these truths purely by faith.

The most powerful truth about Grace, as revealed by the story of the Prodigal Son is this: That there is Grace (and which some people may have as well) but that it is Grace imbued in love. It is one thing to say that your sins are forgiven no matter what they are; it is another to be loved first and then forgiven.

The story of the Prodigal Son teaches us that love precedes forgiveness and proceeds to reconciliation. God loved us and forgave us and made us His friends again. We also ought to forgive others without conditions, but conditionally engage in acts of reconciliation. Forgiveness declares,

---

[132] Romans 6:1-2
[133] See Romans 5:20
[134] Romans 6:6

reconciliation does. If God only forgave us without reconciling us back to Him, we would not be friends. Similarly, if we only forgive people without reconciliation, we would not be friends or be in fellowship with them. Grace has given us both – the power to forgive unconditionally and to reconcile.

This lesson is succinctly captured in the Prodigal Son's story: *"But while he was still a long way off, his father saw him and was filled with compassion for him; he ran to his son, threw his arms around him and kissed him. The son said to him, 'Father, I have sinned against Heaven and against you. I am no longer worthy to be called your son.' But the father said to his servants, 'Quick! Bring the best robe and put it on him. Put a ring on his finger and sandals on his feet. Bring the fattened calf and kill it. Let's have a feast and celebrate…'"*

"But while he was still a long way off, his father saw him and was filled with compassion for him" denotes the act of forgiveness. The son was forgiven even before he asked for it. The father saw his son while the son was far away and he had compassion on him. The son had said nothing and done nothing. That is Grace; it forgives before forgiveness is sought.

However, with reconciliation, the father had to do certain acts. For example, he threw his arms around him and kissed him. He put the best robe on the son. He put a ring on his finger and sandals on his feet.

And finally, they had a fattened calf killed and celebrated in a feast.

Our Lord put it very simply: "Therefore if you are offering your gift at the altar and there remember that your brother has something against you, leave your gift there before the altar. First go and be reconciled to your brother; then come and offer your gift. Reconcile quickly with your adversary, while you are still on the way to court. Otherwise he may hand you over to the judge, and the judge may hand you over to the officer, and you may be thrown into prison."[135] We are forgiven with our active wills involved. However, we must reconcile consciously by doing certain things.

Reconciliation is a form of dispute resolution without the aid of a judge or mediator. It depends on the offender to seek reconciliation from the offended.

Grace is in this, "…and there remember that your brother has something against you…" Grace does not wait for the wrong-doer to ask for forgiveness. Forgiveness may be dispensed even without being asked for. The wronged person may take the initiative and forgive the perpetrator even when the latter has not asked for it or is not willing to ask for it or does not deserve it. Under Law, forgiveness (and reconciliation or restitution) were only possible if the wronged party (the victim) took the

---

[135] Matthew 5:23-25

initiative to exercise it upon the wrongdoer. However, under Grace, the victim and the perpetrator both may take the initiative to exercise forgiveness upon the other without any conditions.

6. Grace Supersedes Law

These two remain: Law and Grace, and the more desirable of them is Grace. We pick up a story in the Book of John:

> The teachers of the law and the Pharisees brought in a woman caught in adultery. They made her stand before the group and said to Jesus, "Teacher, this woman was caught in the act of adultery. In the Law Moses commanded us to stone such women. Now what do you say?" They were using this question as a trap, in order to have a basis for accusing him.
> But Jesus bent down and started to write on the ground with his finger. When they kept on questioning him, he straightened up and said to them, "Let any one of you who is without sin be the first to throw a stone at her." Again, he stooped down and wrote on the ground.
> At this, those who heard began to go away one at a time, the older ones first, until only Jesus was left, with the woman still standing there. Jesus straightened up and asked her,

> "Woman, where are they? Has no one condemned you?" "No one, sir," she said. "Then neither do I condemn you," Jesus declared. "Go now and leave your life of sin."[136]

Here we see an interplay among Law, truth and Grace. The Law was very clear: "In the law, Moses commanded us to stone such women."[137] This woman was caught *in flagrante delicto* or "red-handed." She had broken a law, because having been caught in the act, the truth had been established. The woman did not deny so (which could also have been due to cultural demands). Jesus (who knows everything) does not defend her, either. There is, therefore, irrefutable evidence that she had committed the crime for which she deserved punishment by the dictates of the Mosaic Law. (It is not the intention of this treatise to question why the man with whom she was caught in the act was not brought publicly in the same manner; that is a subject of another lesson). But the passage is enough to provide both context and material facts. The seriousness of this matter was that it was punishable by death.

Therefore, whatever Jesus did next was very important. He could uphold the law – and having established the truth through evidence, the woman would die. Or Jesus

---

[136] John 8:3-11
[137] John 8:5, ESV

would do that which only the judge had the discretion to do, exercise Grace. However, as the passage suggests, Grace could not be imputed in a direct mode as the crowd itself was skeptical about the divinity of Christ. If the Pharisees and teachers of law were convinced that Christ was God, it would have been easier for Christ to simply say, "Daughter, go in peace, your sins are forgiven you." But this situation was complicated. Jesus could not do in this situation what he did in many others. The reason why they brought the woman was to tempt Jesus to acknowledge or deny He was God, that He forgave or did not forgive sins and that He had disregard for the Law of Moses or not.

Here is the brilliance of Jesus' answer. He acknowledged the truth and upheld the Law: "Let any one of you who is without sin be the first to throw a stone at her."[138] In essence, Jesus is saying, "Yes, she is guilty as charged." But he then transferred the responsibility of sin to everyone present. The people understood this. If anyone did throw a stone at her, that person also would be killed in the same way, because he or she would be deserving of the same death. In this way, too, Jesus was equalizing the unequal treatment of woman and men in the Mosaic Law. In other words, the man should be stoned,

---

[138] John 8:7, NIV

too.

Until this event all that Jesus had done was to balance among law, truth and sin. It is what He did next which revealed the power of Grace. First, it was in what Jesus had challenged the crowd, i.e. "Let any one of you who is without sin be the first to throw a stone at her." Jesus challenged them squarely. He, among everyone in the crowd, was the only one without sin. There was overwhelming evidence (truth) that the woman had committed the sin and broken a law.

But Jesus does not accuse her (does not police and prosecute her) and does not condemn her (does not judge her). He pardons her, rewards her with life (instead of death) and gives her the power over sin ("Go now and leave your life of sin"). Indeed, Grace (mercy) will triumph over judgment (sin): "…Mercy triumphs over judgment."[139]

Second and last, it was in this statement, "Has no-one condemned you….Then neither do I condemn you." Here is the Grace of our Lord Jesus Christ. No-one condemned the woman. That is, no-one who was a sinner and who did not deserve to condemn her, because they all had sinned and came short of the glory of God.[140] However, Jesus had no sin, had

---

[139] James 2:13b
[140] Romans 3:23

never sinned and as the Creator, He had the power to condemn sin and the sinner. Yet, He reserved His divine right under the Law to condemn and punish sinners. He, rather, exercised mercy to pardon and forgive sin. He forgave the woman not because of the same reason that everyone else did. He did not let the woman go without being condemned because He had sinned like all others who left the woman alone. No. He forgave the woman because of Grace. She did not deserve to be forgiven. She did not deserve to be pardoned. She did not deserve to be let go free. She had sinned. And according to Mosaic Law, the woman deserved condemnation and punishment (death). Yet, the Lord of Grace had mercy on her and simply released her to go free and unpunished.

Grace pardons unconditionally. However, Grace provides a conditional requirement to live a sinless life. God will forgive everyone who comes to Him. Grace will not count a person's former sins. Grace will not require a record of wrongs. However, after forgiveness, the person must go and "sin no more." Grace is not weak on sin nor does it tolerate sin; Grace provides the power over sin: "For the grace of God has appeared, bringing salvation to all men. It instructs us to renounce ungodliness and worldly passions, and to live sensible, upright, and godly lives in the present age, as we await the blessed hope and glorious appearance of our great God and Savior, Jesus Christ.[141]

In this verse, we are informed that Grace is our instructor. Grace re-orients us into the ways of righteousness, uprightness, holiness and blamelessness. Grace teaches us to denounce sin and evil. It coaches us to live pure Christian lives. It teaches us to live blameless in a fallen world. Without Grace, we are powerless over sin. Without Grace, we are just as weak as anyone was under the Law. However, with Grace, we are on a journey "…until we all reach unity in the faith and in the knowledge of the Son of God and become mature, attaining to the whole measure of the fullness of Christ."[142] As the Bible also tells us that, "From His fullness we have all received grace upon grace."[143] Grace guides us towards maturity in Christ among the mature, however, we speak a message of wisdom - but not the wisdom of this age or of the rulers of this age, who are coming to nothing.[144] Brothers, stop thinking like children. In regard to evil be infants, but in your thinking be mature.[145] Paul admonishes his children, "…for whom I am again in the pains of childbirth until Christ is formed in

---

[141] Titus 2:11-13
[142] Ephesians 4:13
[143] John 1:16
[144] 1 Corinthians 2:6
[145] 1 Corinthians 14:20

you."[146] And for the Ephesians, he intercedes, "…asking that the God of our Lord Jesus Christ, the glorious Father, may give you a spirit of wisdom and revelation in your knowledge of Him."[147]

Grace is Christ's substitute on earth. Grace's mandate is until Christ reappears in His Second Coming. As long as Christ has not yet reappeared, Grace will do what Christ personally could have been doing. It keeps us in Christ until Christ comes. Grace, therefore, has a span. It will end when Christ returns.

> O, grace, gracious grace
> How you have been to me, kind
> O, grace, generous grace,
> I have in you a dear friend, find.
> I love you, grace,
> I really, really love your face.

Getting back to our text,[148] in this story, Grace triumphs. The question Jesus asks also reveals a very important fact, that the woman's accusers were powerless under the heavy weight of sin. Surely, if they were sinless or righteous by the Law, they would have stoned the woman. The Law does not make anyone righteous before God. In fact, it is the Law which even makes them aware of their sins. And since everyone who is

---

[146] Galatians 4:19
[147] Ephesians 1:17
[148] See John 8:3-11, *supra*.

with sin cannot approach God, it is only through the gracious imputing of righteousness on us through Grace by faith that we can please God and be found worthy to inherit, to share in His inheritance:

> Therefore no one will be declared righteous in God's sight by the works of the law; rather, through the law we become conscious of our sin. But now apart from the law the righteousness of God has been made known, to which the Law and the Prophets testify. This righteousness is given through faith in Jesus Christ to all who believe. There is no difference between Jew and Gentile, for all have sinned and fall short of the glory of God, and all are justified freely by his grace through the redemption that came by Christ Jesus.[149]

They brought the woman to Grace and truth. Jesus is the Word of God which became flesh, and not only that, it was God in flesh full of Grace and truth: "The Word became flesh and made his dwelling among us. We have seen his glory, the glory of the one and only Son, who came from the Father, full of grace and truth."[150] Indeed,

---

[149] Romans 3:20-24
[150] John 1:14

> How can it be, that at the point of grace
> Here they lay the sin-buttered woman,
> Her accusers, in shambles and guiltiness
> One by one left her mute by the Word Man!

And you did not appreciate the power of Grace until you considered this. These Pharisees and the teachers of the law. This crowd of people and, indeed, this woman, for them, within a pace of few weeks, Christ would go on the cross to die. For the one who accused the woman, He would die. For the accused woman, He would die. And for the cheering crowd, He would also die. He, who was the only righteous among them, for the unrighteous He would die: "But God commendeth his love toward us, in that, while we were yet sinners, Christ died for us."[151] God gave proof of His love to us in Christ's dying for us while we were still sinners. There is no further proof than that.

It is important to note the relationship among glory, Grace and truth. Christ, according to John,[152] came from the Father (from Heaven). However, it is not the brilliance, the firmament of Heaven that

---

[151] Romans 5:8
[152] John 1:14

Christ's glory emanates. It is as the author says, "We have seen the glory…"[153] Christ did not come in power and splendor: "He grew up before him like a tender shoot, and like a root out of dry ground. He had no beauty or majesty to attract us to him, nothing in his appearance that we should desire him."[154] And Paul makes this explicit: "Who, existing in the form of God, did not consider equality with God something to be grasped, but emptied Himself, taking the form of a servant, being made in human likeness. And being found in appearance as a man, He humbled Himself and became obedient to death—even death on a cross."[155] In appearance, Christ was just like all of us, "So He had to be made like His brothers in every way, that He might become a merciful and faithful high priest in service to God, in order to make atonement for the sins of the people."[156]

So, what glory did they or us see in Christ? Paul clarifies: "There is one glory of the sun, and another glory of the moon, and another glory of the stars; for star differs from star in glory."[157] Glory or splendor is relative. But in each of the instances referred to here, it has to do with the degree of splendor. By analogy, Christ's glory has

---

[153] John 1:14
[154] Isaiah 53:2
[155] Philippians 2:6-8
[156] Hebrews 2:17
[157] 1 Corinthians 15:41

its own nature. It is revealed in His Grace and truth: "So the Word became human and made his home among us. He was full of unfailing love and faithfulness. And we have seen his glory, the glory of the Father's one and only Son, full of grace and truth."[158] And again, "For the Law was given through Moses; Grace and truth came through Jesus Christ."[159]

From the above, two truths emerge. First, John tells us that Christ became flesh and dwelt among us. In order words, Christ became Jesus; became a human being like us and dwelt on earth. We know that His birth, though miraculous, was nothing extraordinary. He was born in a manger. Although the angels celebrated His birth, there was nothing "glorious" about His appearance.

Second and finally, there must be something about His qualities that made His birth "full of glory." Apostle John tell us that it was Grace and truth. His unfailing love, His unmerited favor towards us and His faithfulness and truth made Jesus our Lord glorious. It is the ultimate defining mark of His being. John says, "We have seen his glory." Indeed, they saw His Grace in operation. They saw the exposition of the truth in action. They saw the fullness of His glory.

---

[158] John 1:14, *supra*.
[159] John 1:17

Indeed, the Law was given through a human agent, Moses. But when it came to Grace, God took on the form of a human being and delivered it to earth by Himself. The import of this is revolutionary. A good example is to paint a royal picture. Kings and queens rarely herald their own missives; they have agents who deliver the message. However, from time to time, kings and queens may deliver the message by themselves if the message is very important. With the Law, God sent Moses. With Grace, He sent His Only Begotten Son. The message of Grace was too important to be delivered via a human agent.

God brought us Grace by Himself. And we saw the glory of His Grace in operation: That, of course, was Him forgiving sins unconditionally, healing the sick, raising the dead, comforting the weak, cheering the weary, calling the feeble and the nonentities, speaking to and dining with sinners, washing His own servants' feet, loving the unloved, breaking bread with His disciples, praying for His enemies, rebuking the hypocrites, sharing food with the hungry, paying taxes, breaking tribal lines, and even dying for those who did not deserve it – all of us! That is the beauty, the power, and the glory of Grace.

7. In-Christ Sinless Perfection

Believers in Christ through faith, have

sinless perfection. This is not through works, lest any person should boast.[160] Grace commends us to the perfection of Christ. Under Grace, justification is only possible by faith, not by works: "Know that a person is not justified by the works of the law, but by faith in Jesus Christ. So, we, too, have put our faith in Christ Jesus that we may be justified by faith in Christ and not by the works of the law, *because by the works of the law no one will be justified*."[161]

The very notion that you are justified by faith should send a divine chill into your human spines. The best illustration is to ask a group of athletes to a racing match. And the only qualification is that they cannot run. Or to ask a group of chefs to a cooking contest and the only qualification is that they cannot cook. Or to ask musicians to a competitive concert and the only qualification is that they cannot play. Or to ask a choir of singers to a singing symposium and the only condition is that they cannot sing. Under Grace, it is the unqualified who are qualified. It sounds like an oxymoron, because it is. There is no quality that qualifies under Grace. Lack of any particular quality qualifies us under Grace. That is what is meant by the fact that we are justified by faith. Justification, in nature, involves proving something, and, of

---

[160] See Ephesians 2:8-9
[161] Galatians 2:16 (emphasis added)

course, that means demonstrating, showing, acting or doing something. Under Grace, justification involves simply believing that we are righteous. This obvious simplicity is mindboggling. And yet, that is what Grace has done. We ought not prove anything, demonstrate anything, qualify for anything or display any qualities – simply believing, simply having faith.

We have been justified by faith. Justification, by definition, involves removing something and replacing it with another. God could not just remove something from us but He had, of necessity, to give us something else in its place.

God removed guilt and the penalty of sin through the death of His Son. He also declared a sinner righteous by the same token, through Christ's atoning sacrifice. To understand this thesis, it is important to remember that God calls us to the same righteousness standard He called His Son to. To inherit the Kingdom of God, we have to be pure just as He is pure; holy just as He is holy; and blameless just as He is blameless. God does not, and will not change, lower or compromise His standard. We have to meet the exact standard to which He called His Son. Jesus, too, called us to the same standard as His Father is: "Be perfect, therefore, as your heavenly

Father is perfect."[162]

The standard God calls us to is the perfection standard. This is literally, not figuratively. In other words, we are called to be pure – without any sin. We are called to live a life that is one hundred percent without blame or fault. We are called to a daily cleaned life – no vile from our mouths, no malice in our hearts, and no guilt in our actions. We are called to love all, hate none, and worship only God.

No human being can meet the above standard, no-one born of a woman. However, God has made us perfect through His Son Jesus Christ. God, through Grace, sees us through His Son, not through our own lenses. Christ lived a perfect life for us, so that we might not have to live a perfect life. Christ committed no sin, so that God could accept us. Christ is our perfection, and that is Grace. If God should put us to the standard of righteousness without Christ, no-one would be saved. And how did Christ Jesus do this?

First, "[Jesus Christ] committed no sin, neither was deceit found in his mouth."[163]

Second, "For we do not have a high priest who is unable to sympathize with our weaknesses, but one who in every respect has been tempted as we are, yet without sin."[164]

---

[162] Matthew 5:48
[163] 1 Peter 2:22
[164] Hebrews 4:15

Third, "For our sake he made him to be sin who knew no sin, so that in him we might become the righteousness of God."[165]

Fourth, "You know that he appeared to take away sins, and in him there is no sin."[166]

Fifth, "How much more will the blood of Christ, who through the eternal Spirit offered himself without blemish to God, purify our conscience from dead works to serve the living God."[167]

Sixth, "But with the precious blood of Christ, like that of a lamb without blemish or spot."[168]

Seventh, "For God has done what the law, weakened by the flesh, could not do. By sending his own Son in the likeness of sinful flesh and for sin, he condemned sin in the flesh…"[169]

Eighth, "Although he was a son, he learned obedience through what he suffered. And being made perfect, he became the source of eternal salvation to all who obey him…"[170]

Ninth, "Which one of you convicts me of sin? If I tell the truth, why do you not believe me?"[171]

---

[165] 2 Corinthians 5:21
[166] 1 John 3:5
[167] Hebrews 9:14
[168] 1 Peter 1:19
[169] Romans 8:3
[170] Hebrews 5:8-9
[171] John 8:46

And tenth, "Pilate said to him, 'What is truth?' After he had said this, he went back outside to the Jews and told them, 'I find no guilt in him…'"[172]

The above, are the few illustrations of the perfection of Christ. He is the only *human being* who never sinned. All of us have sinned and stand condemned: "…for all have sinned and fall short of the glory of God…"[173] The implications of this verse are chilling. It fundamentally means that no-one could enter the Kingdom of God. In reality, no-one can even come near God. Sin separated us from God. Man is unable by himself to reach God. By himself, man cannot even pray or do anything that God could accept.

The Law was an attempt at reaching perfection through human efforts. Instead of creating a perfect person, it only made people miserable. The more people knew they were sinful and could not do anything about it, the more miserable they became. Law strengthened sin, not weakening it.

How could, therefore, humans be perfect just as God is? There was only one way, through substitutional death. One perfect Man, Jesus, should fulfill the requirements of the Law for the entire human race. Christ came to fulfill the Law on our behalf: "Do not think that I have

---

[172] John 18:38
[173] Romans 3:23

come to abolish the Law or the Prophets; I have not come to abolish them but to fulfill them. For I assure you and most solemnly say to you, until Heaven and earth pass away, not the smallest letter or stroke [of the pen] will pass from the Law until all things are accomplished."[174] Christ said He came to fulfill the Law, and He did: "Christ is the culmination of the law so that there may be righteousness for everyone who believes."[175]

In other words, Christ has already accomplished the purpose for which the Law was given. As a result, all who believe in Him are made right with God. If they are right with God, then they are, through Christ, also perfect as God is. Through Christ, they have obeyed the Law.

8. A Sealed Inheritance

We have been sealed for an inheritance. A seal is a legal apparatus. A seal warrants that the promisor will perform according to the stipulation. It binds the promisor. Most seals are endorsed by those in authority and they bind them to carry out as promised. A seal signifies ownership, guarantees security and is a mark of authenticity. God has guaranteed believers the highest endorsement of them all:

---

[174] Matthew 5:17-18
[175] Romans 10:4

> Praise be to the God and Father of our Lord Jesus Christ, who has blessed us in the heavenly realms with every spiritual blessing in Christ….And in Him you were sealed with the promised Holy Spirit, having heard and believed the word of truth, the gospel of your salvation. The Spirit is the pledge of our inheritance until the redemption of those who are God's possession, to the praise of His glory.…[176]

There are three issues here: What is the seal all about? Who is the symbol of the seal? And what are the benefits of the seal?

The seal is about our inheritance. The Holy Spirit is the guarantee with which we have been sealed. The benefit of this inheritance is such that all that Christ has inherited has become ours as well. We have inherited God Himself, the world, and the resurrection. In Christ, we have become one with God, we have kissed the Son, "Kiss his son, or he will be angry and your way will lead to your destruction, for his wrath can flare up in a moment. Blessed are all who take refuge in him."[177] We have averted destruction, God is happy with us, and we have taken refuge in Him. We have

---

[176] Ephesians 1:3, 13-14
[177] Psalm 2:12

all spiritual blessings in God as our own,[178] and one day, after the resurrection, we shall inherit the world: "Blessed are the meek, for they will inherit the earth."[179]

Some people think that we shall go to "Heaven" above, that is only partly true. Heaven will come to earth:

> Then I saw a new Heaven
> and a new earth, for the first
> heaven and earth had passed away,
> and the sea was no more. I saw
> the holy city, the new Jerusalem,
> coming down out of Heaven from
> God, prepared as a bride adorned
> for her husband. And I heard a
> loud voice from the throne saying:
> 'Behold, the dwelling place of God
> is with man, and He will live with
> them. They will be His people,
> and God Himself will be with
> them as their God.…[180]

The word used here is "new" or a remake, not a recreation. God is not going to do away with the elemental set-up as is today, He will merely purge the old formations so that a new one is carved. Our earth will undergo a renewal, not a total recreation. This present world will burn as with fire, and the result will be a rebranded earth, not another creation. We are not going

---

[178] Ephesians 1:3
[179] Matthew 5:5
[180] Revelation 21: 1-3

anywhere. We will temporarily be suspended in the heavenlies waiting for the New Jerusalem. To a new and renewed earth, we shall return. The beauty of all this is that God will live with us and there will be no longer any sea.

Grace has given us access to all these. We can illustrate this simply. Imagine you are a very poor bride getting married to a very rich groom. Immediately the vows are exchanged and he adds you to a join-bank account, you become a partaker of his inheritance. In the absence of a prenuptial agreement to the contrary, you can cash in all the money in his bank account, because it is also your money now. So, God has added us to His account, and we are equal heirs with Christ: "Now if we are children, then we are heirs – heirs of God and co-heirs with Christ, if indeed we share in his sufferings in order that we may also share in his glory."[181]

We did not go to the cross with Christ, but we share in His suffering (and we symbolize this with the Communion) by faith. We will also share in His glory in the same way. That is why even if we were to suffer presently, "I consider that our present sufferings are not worth comparing with the glory that will be revealed in us."[182] We have an inheritance in Christ, a great

---

[181] Romans 8:17
[182] Romans 8:18

reward. Under Grace, our rewards are now based on Grace, not effort or works. Our quality of work is rewarded for love, and not skill.

If anyone wants to work hard in Grace, there is a place for it. In Hebrews, Scripture demands that those who seek God must do so diligently.[183] Diligence means hard work. The only labor we must do with all hard work is seeking God. How do we do this? Since we cannot see God Himself, seeking God diligently might mean serving others: "Each of you should use whatever gift you have received to serve others, as faithful stewards of God's grace in its various forms."[184] Under the new dispensation of Grace, no-one should stay idly, but must be actively sharing: "But to each one of us grace has been given as Christ apportioned it."[185] We should use Grace to perform wonders: "Now Stephen, a man full of God's grace and power, performed great wonders and signs among the people."[186]

Grace gives us strength, not rituals or sacrifices: "Do not be carried away by all kinds of strange teachings. It is good for our hearts to be strengthened by grace, not by eating ceremonial foods, which is of no benefit to those who do so."[187] For those

---

[183] Heb. 11:1,6
[184] 1 Peter 4:10
[185] Ephesians 4:7
[186] Acts 6:8
[187] Hebrews 13:9

who preach, deliver Good News with deep Grace: "Paul, a servant of Christ Jesus, called to be an apostle and set apart for the gospel of God— the gospel he promised beforehand through his prophets in the Holy Scripture regarding his Son, who as to his earthly life was a descendant of David, and who through the Spirit of holiness was appointed the Son of God in power by his resurrection from the dead: Jesus Christ our Lord. Through him we received grace and apostleship to call all the Gentiles to the obedience that comes from faith for his name's sake."[188]

Through Grace, we have favor with all people, and we can gain everything: "She was taken to King Xerxes in the royal residence in the tenth month, the month of Tebeth, in the seventh year of his reign. Now the king was attracted to Esther more than to any of the other women, and she won his favor and approval more than any of the other virgins. So he set a royal crown on her head and made her queen instead of Vashti."[189]

We no longer labor for salvation, we receive it by Grace through faith in Christ Jesus: "For it is by grace you have been saved, through faith—and this is not from yourselves, it is the gift of God— not by

---

[188] Romans 1:1-5
[189] Esther 2:16-17

works, so that no one can boast."[190]

We increase Grace and peace as we learn about and know our Lord Jesus Christ more and more: "Grace and peace be yours in abundance through the knowledge of God and of Jesus our Lord."[191] More Grace is also given to the humble, the proud will be vigorously opposed by God. That is why Scripture says: "God opposes the proud but shows favor to the humble."[192] And more importantly, hard work under this dispensation is defined as Grace: "But by the grace of God I am what I am: and his grace which [was bestowed] upon me was not in vain; but I labored more abundantly than they all: yet not I, but the grace of God which was with me."[193]

In Summary

God gives us Grace to do whatever we do for Him; it is not our own strength. No-one should ever boast of anything God has allowed them to do – whether by way of talent, abilities, service or gifts – it's all by Grace, otherwise it is by works. Grace has not forestalled us from all boasts. It has empowered us to know God and in that

---

[190] See Ephesians 2:8-9; see also Titus 2:11 and Acts 15:11
[191] 2 Peter 1:2
[192] James 4:6
[193] 1 Corinthians 15:10

alone we should boast: "But let the one who boasts boast about this: That they have the understanding to know me, that I am the LORD, who exercises kindness, justice and righteousness on earth, for in these I delight, declares the LORD."[194] And this has not changed irrespective of eras or milieus.

> O Lord, my God, grace has written
> Through my hands, grace has given
> Grace sharpened all my faculties
> And made easy all my difficulties.

---

[194] Jeremiah 9:24

5 | THE FAITH FACTOR

In this chapter, we highlight how faith factors in all aspects of divine encounters, interactions and interventions. Two thematic premises will be rested, namely, that faith is necessary to the access of divine and spiritual accruals by the mortals; and because, by faith, believers have died and rose with Christ, they can lay claim to all benefits accrued to them by virtue of inheritance by Grace.

Faith – An Only Channel to Spiritual Blessings

We turn to the topic that has been vicariously covered throughout this text. Stated factually, there is no Grace without faith. This is because faith makes Grace available. Faith is necessary to access the benefits of Grace. The new spiritual dispensation is always by Grace through faith. But it is even more.

Faith is not just a topical issue in Christianity, it is also an absolute requirement everywhere there is an interaction between the mortals and the immortals, temporal and divine, and earthly and spiritual. Take as an illustration our understanding of matter. We now know that it manifests into three states, namely, solids, liquids and gasses. We are capable of manipulating and accessing solids and liquids through the five senses of taste, sight, smell, hearing and feeling. We may have challenges using all the five senses to manipulate or access gasses, but we have indirect methodologies of doing so, usually through our feeling and smell. Some gasses may be tasted and even heard.

But humans have no way of accessing the spiritual except through faith. It is no wonder religion is sometimes referred to as *the* Faith. This does not discriminate whether one is a believer in Christ, belongs to a religion or not, or knows what they are doing or not. It is an established universal principle. Those who wish to seek the intervention of the spiritual world from the material world must do so through faith. Faith, therefore, connects the spiritual elements to the material, earthly beings. Indeed, "Faith is this extraordinary principle which links man to God."[195] Whether that element be God, gods or angels, faith is required to interact with them. God has specifically required that everything done or that is incidental to Him, must be by faith. "For whatever does not proceed from faith is sin."[196] And those

---

[195] Martyn Lloyd Jones
[196] Romans 14:23

who come to Him by faith will make Him happy or pleased.[197]

Christ Died; Believers Died

In Chapter 4, we discussed, "A Sealed Inheritance." Through Grace by faith, those who believe in Christ have become the beneficiaries of God's blessings and fruitfulness sealed under the Abrahamic Covenant. God had bequeathed to Abraham the promise, thus:

> Then you will not be sluggish, but will imitate those who through faith and patience inherit what has been promised. When God made His promise to Abraham, since He had no one greater to swear by, He swore by Himself, saying, "I will surely bless you and multiply your descendants."[198]

This piece of Scripture brings all the facets needed for a legally-sanctioned deed or codicil to be enforceable at law. Assuming that the principles of Family Law under Common-law jurisprudence apply, it will follow that God is the promisor, who left a sworn Will for His would-be children. As established earlier, He first adopted us as

---

[197] See Hebrews 11, esp. verse 6
[198] Hebrews 6:12-14

His own children: "He predestined us for adoption to sonship through Jesus Christ, in accordance with his pleasure and will."[199] Sons also includes *daughters*. The qualification into being adopted as God's children is first, by faith: "But to all who did receive Him, to those who believed in His name, He gave the right to become children of God—children born not of blood, nor of the desire or will of man, but born of God,"[200] and then by being led by God's Holy Spirit: "For all who are led by the Spirit of God are sons of God."[201]

Divine providence has facilitated that these two take place side by side or contemporaneously. For those who believe in Jesus Christ also receive the gift of the Holy Spirit or become entitled to this reception.[202] Believers in Christ become entitled to everything God is and God has, just like children born into a family are entitled to everything in the household.

God is a master planner; He did not allow His Son to die without a Will. In other words, our Lord Jesus Christ did not die intestate or without a Will. He has

---

[199] Ephesians 1:5
[200] John 1:12-13
[201] Romans 8:14
[202] Theological dispositions differ on which grace is received first, salvation or the baptism of or in the Holy Spirit. In practice, however, it does not matter what the order is; God in His wisdom has provided for a way in which both are experienced by a believing soul.

spoken in many places on His desire of how His estate should be distributed. His estate includes the world: "The earth is the LORD's, and everything in it, the world, and all who live in it;"[203] all wealth, "The silver is mine, and the gold is mine, saith the LORD of hosts;"[204] all animals, "For all the animals of the forest are mine, and I own the cattle on a thousand hills;"[205] His Kingdom, "Do not be afraid, little flock, for your Father is pleased to give you the kingdom;"[206] and, of course, God Himself: "And since we are his children, we are his heirs. In fact, together with Christ we are heirs of God."[207] The last two are immeasurable: We have been given a part in God's glory and Kingdom – that means everything. That is the extent of our inheritance through faith in Christ Jesus, our Lord.

The Holy Spirit Guarantees the Inheritance

At the Day of Pentecost, God sent the Holy Spirit following the resurrection of our Lord Jesus Christ. God (Jesus Christ) wrote the Will, and God appointed the Holy Spirit to be the administrator – He has

---

[203] Psalm 24:1; see also Deuteronomy 10:14; Exodus 9:29; and 1 Corinthians 10:26
[204] Haggai 2:8
[205] Psalm 50:10
[206] Luke 12:32
[207] Romans 8:17

the letters of administration to distribute God's estate to those who believe in Jesus Christ. The Holy Spirit is also the executor of the Will. This is most eloquently stated in Ephesians: "The Spirit is God's guarantee that he will give us the inheritance he promised and that he has purchased us to be his own people. He did this so we would praise and glorify him."[208] The words "guarantee" or "guarantor" or "pledge" are an equitable rendition of administrator or executor. All these apply to the Holy Spirit in the New Testament.

Basic to the law of Wills and administration of testate estates is the fact that the testator or the person who made the Will must die. And equally central to inheritance law is the fact that the beneficiary should not have been the one who caused the death of the testator. It is clear in Scripture that, Jesus Christ, the testator, died. Two verses of Scripture are highlighted here, and which also form the predominant thesis of the doctrines both of estate acquisition and testate testimonial. The first is: "Christ Jesus who died—more than that, who was raised to life—is at the right hand of God and is also interceding for us,"[209] and the second is like it: "The death he died, he died to sin once for all; but the life he lives, he lives to God. In the

---

[208] Ephesians 1:14
[209] Romans 8:34

same way, count yourselves dead to sin but alive to God in Christ Jesus."[210]

The Three Premises

In these verses, three premises have been established. First, the testator died. And this is important "because a will does not take effect until the one who made it has died; it cannot be executed while he is still alive."[211] Because Jesus Christ died, this necessarily invoked the rights of the beneficiaries to the estate.

Second, and the most complicated part of Jesus Christ's death, is that beneficiaries have been implicated in it. The very people he had named as beneficiaries demanded that He be crucified, and that is all of us, vicariously: "And though they found no ground for a death sentence, they asked Pilate to have Him executed."[212] In essence, this excluded all of us from sharing into God's inheritance. However, due to His love and mercy, God adopted us as His own children, which gave us access to His estate. But he did one more very important act, Christ rose again from the dead. This meant that the inheritance became ours by

---

[210] Romans 6:8-11
[211] Hebrews 9:17
[212] Acts 13:28; see also Matthew 27:16-26, Mark 15:7-15, Luke 23:18-25, and John 18:40

right and attestation. By right because He died, and by attestation because He rose from the dead to "mediate,"[213] "witness"[214] and "represent"[215] us should any conflicts arise in relation to our entitlement to the inheritance. Since in Christ Jesus dwells all the fullness of the Godhead,[216] it is reasonable to conclude that Jesus Christ is the testator whose death puts His own Will into effect. In essence, Jesus Christ ratified the New Covenant for those who believe in Him with His own blood (death).

And third, "count yourselves dead to sin but alive to God in Christ Jesus."[217] This is a revolutionary statement. Not only did Jesus Christ die, but we, through Him, also died. The dead have the following rights: All debts, liabilities and faults against them are automatically cancelled. The only thing the dead take with them is their records of wrongs. However, this, too, was dealt with in Christ. The New Living Translation renders Romans 3:21-27 this way:

> But now God has shown us a way to be made right with him without keeping the requirements of the law, as was promised in the writings of Moses[a] and the

---

[213] See 1 Timothy 2:5
[214] See 1 Timothy 2:5
[215] Romans 8:34, *ibid*.
[216] See Colossians 2:9 or Romans 1:20
[217] Romans 6:8-11, *ibid*.

prophets long ago. We are made right with God by placing our faith in Jesus Christ. And this is true for everyone who believes, no matter who we are. For everyone has sinned; we all fall short of God's glorious standard. Yet God, in his grace, freely makes us right in his sight. He did this through Christ Jesus when he freed us from the penalty for our sins. For God presented Jesus as the sacrifice for sin. People are made right with God when they believe that Jesus sacrificed his life, shedding his blood. This sacrifice shows that God was being fair when he held back and did not punish those who sinned in times past, for he was looking ahead and including them in what he would do in this present time. God did this to demonstrate his righteousness, for he himself is fair and just, and he makes sinners right in his sight when they believe in Jesus. Can we boast, then, that we have done anything to be accepted by God? No, because our acquittal is not based on obeying the law. It is based on faith. So we are made right with God through faith and not by obeying the law.

The argument is rested here. Grace has also pardoned all our faults, and cleared our records of wrongs permanently through Christ. Sin has been permanently forgiven – all it takes is confessing this reality: "If we confess our sins, he is faithful and just and will forgive us our sins and purify us from all unrighteousness."[218] All that the spiritual process requires, is for the recipients of Grace to *admit* or *acknowledge* their sinful state of affairs and what Christ Jesus has already done for them through the Cross. He has forgiven their sins and if they confess so, they are exonerated.

To those who believe in Jesus Christ, there is no longer any judgment for wrongs. They have passed from judgment to life: "Very truly I tell you, whoever hears my word and believes him who sent me has eternal life and will not be judged but has crossed over from death to life."[219] Grace has eliminated any form of condemnation based on past sins and misdeeds; those who perish do so by choice: "Whoever believes in Him is not condemned, but whoever does not believe has already been condemned, because he has not believed in the name of God's one and only Son."[220] Under Grace, obedience to the law is no longer the standard for salvation. Those who believe in Christ Jesus have been acquitted of all their sins and the future

---

[218] 1 John 1:9
[219] John 5:24
[220] John 3:18

punishment has been removed even before they obey a single jot. They are dead, and, therefore, no condemnation from Satan can affect them. Grace has made believers untouchable by any venom of sin or the power of death.[221]

In Conclusion

Grace is the state of our current spiritual position. Faith makes Grace work. So, by Grace through faith, we have access to all spiritual blessings, including God Himself. We have been adopted into sonship and forgiven of our sins, including our being accomplices in the crucifixion of Christ and the Adamic fall. By Grace, we have been left with a Will, and by faith, we have inherited life, the world, God's Kingdom and God Himself. Christ protects our accruals through His intercessory work on the right hand of the Father, and the Holy Spirit guarantees them.

> How can it be, that the temporal be immortalized
> Serve for the grace that through faith works
> How should I be a subject of divinity moralized

---

[221] See 1 Corinthians 15:55-57

Serve that His death for me a bliss it makes.

6 | GOSPEL AND GRACE

Grace Saves

In Acts, we read, "On the contrary, we believe it is through the grace of the Lord Jesus that we are saved, just as they are."[222]

In the past, God had made a distinction between the Jews and Gentiles. He had chosen the Jews purely by Grace, but He dealt with them according to Law. Rabbi Alan Lurie agrees:

> Jews were chosen to bring to the world this message of goodness: treat the stranger as one's own, love your fellow as yourself, care for the widow, orphan and handicapped, give to the poor, know that Spirit is higher than material success and that you are a child of God, and most importantly, always value life. In this way, Jews are chosen to be the lamp that allows God's light to shine in the world.[223]

---

[222] Acts 15:11
[223] Rabbi Alan Lurie, "What Does It Mean that the Jews are God's Chosen People?" *The HuffPost*, January 23rd, 2014

But the Grace imputed upon the Jews was different from that which was brought through Christ. The Jews were chosen by God and they were tested. That test was fulfilled through Abraham. The first man, Adam, disobeyed God and failed the first test of faith. Abraham believed God and through him all the Jews became accepted as a unique race of people: "So also Abraham 'believed God, and it was credited to him as righteousness.'"[224] And through the paterfamilias Abraham, God was establishing a new way of gaining righteousness by faith.

However, the righteousness imputed upon the Jews through Abraham had limitations, although he was the father of all those who believe and are saved. The greatest limitation was that Abraham himself, like Adam, had flaws; Abraham had sin. God would tolerate this imperfect state of righteousness until He had provided a better way. Before a better way was revealed, God would use the Law as a schoolmaster preparing the would-be recipients of the new Grace: "Wherefore the law was our schoolmaster to bring us unto Christ, that we might be justified by faith."[225] The Law, as it were, was a guardian or a trainer. It was in place to ward for the time when Grace would be revealed.

---

[224] Galatians 3:6
[225] Galatians 3:24

When Christ came, the age of Law ended. Christ brought Grace. He was both sinless[226] and perfect, and His dispensation would secure for all people (Jews and Gentiles), once for all, the righteousness that is of Grace through faith in Him: "Christ is the end of the Law, in order to bring righteousness to everyone who believes."[227] After Christ came, they graduated from being under tutelage of the Law to being free and able to exercise their new freedom of Grace by faith in Christ: "Now that faith has come, we are no longer under a guardian."[228]

Now, all those who were before Abraham, those who were Abraham's offspring and those who obtained righteousness by faith through the example of Abraham, have been fused together in the ultimate gift, Christ:

> Therefore, the promise comes by faith, so that it may rest on grace and may be guaranteed to all Abraham's offspring – not only to those who are of the Law, but also to those who are of the faith of Abraham. He is the father of us

---

[226] Online dictionary defines sinless as "free from sin." However, this term is used loosely as sinless, as in "sin-less" as opposed to "sin-more." Sinless may not connote the same meaning as "without sin." In this case, the latter is preferred.
[227] Romans 10:4
[228] Galatians 3:25

all."[229] Abraham is the father of all those who believe for redemption. As it is said, "It is because of Him that you are in Christ Jesus, who has become for us wisdom from God: our righteousness, holiness, and redemption.[230]

Ultimately, it is not the faith of Abraham that saves; it is the Grace of God through faith in Christ which saves; "In Him we have redemption through His blood, the forgiveness of our trespasses, according to the riches of His grace."[231] Through the Law, God was actively preparing humanity for righteousness; through Abraham, He was sending humanity a message that, that righteousness would be of faith through Grace.

The Sin Dilemma

Sin had brought a serious dilemma. First, it was a volitional choice of people. Satan simply tempted humanity to not believe God. Humanity disobeyed God because of unbelief. Satan did not sin for humanity. Satan's initial sin of pride was not instigated by a third party; he simply developed sin of his own will. However, for humanity, sin was as a result of a trickster. Humanity was

---

[229] Romans 4:16
[230] 1 Corinthians 1:30
[231] Ephesians 1:7

duped into sinning. Man (and woman) gave up their will to be right with God through a tempter.

Second, by falling into Satan's trap, man would be willingly surrendering his dominion of the earth to Satan. Man gave his dominion as a gift to Satan. This pre-empted God of the power to forcefully take back the dominion from Satan. Being sinful, man had also lost the power to conquer evil. To be able to regain his power over sin, man had to succumb to high justice. Man must die because the wages of sin is death. Indeed, "The soul who sins shall die…"[232] Man[233] had to succumb to the Law of Death. He had to die as punishment for his sin.

This is where the fundamental power of Grace begins. God did not allow man to be punished for his sin. God would be punished for man's sin, instead: "God made him who had no sin to be sin for us, so that in him we might become the righteousness of God."[234] This statement is one of the greatest statements in the whole of the universe. This is the quintessence of Grace. That meant three things:

The first thing was that God would become man. The Creator would have to be born as a human being – with all limitations of the physical reality. God did that: "But

---

[232] Ezekiel 18:20a
[233] Also means women
[234] 2 Corinthians 5:21

when the time had fully come, God sent His Son, born of a woman, born under the Law, to redeem those under the Law, that we might receive our adoption as sons."[235]

The second thing was that through this process of incarnation, God would be less than angels. It is the state of the lowest humility God could have ever undergone: "Who, existing in the form of God, did not consider equality with God something to cling to, but emptied Himself, taking the form of a servant, being made in human likeness."[236]

And the third thing was that as a man, God had to be exposed to the lowest form of death, the death of the lowest criminal: "And being found in appearance as a man, He humbled Himself and became obedient to death—even death on a cross."[237]

The three above, made every instinct in the devil to smile. God is dead? The world would finally belong to Satan, permanently. The devil's objective to mankind was: Pay the price and die. No God in His right mind would dare to do that. Even when Satan knew Jesus was God, he least expected that one-day Satan would be given permission to kill God. He could not believe his fortune when on that fateful Calvary day, Jesus was forsaken by His Father: "About three in the afternoon Jesus

---

[235] Galatians 4:4
[236] Philippians 2:6-7
[237] Philippians 2:8

cried out in a loud voice, 'Eli, Eli, lama sabachthani?' (which means 'My God, my God, why have you forsaken me?'"[238]

In that hour, Satan had to strike with ephemeral precision. He finally had the only rarest chance, one chance, to kill God, his Creator. He did. But God had a plan for resurrection. This was discussed among the Holy Trinity. How do we know this? The following passage illustrate:

> Therefore, my heart is glad and my glory rejoices; My flesh also will dwell securely. For You will not abandon my soul to Sheol; Nor will You allow Your Holy One to undergo decay. You will make known to me the path of life; In Your presence is fullness of joy; In Your right hand, there are pleasures forever....[239]

Jesus rejoiced when He was assured that He would be raised again ("my glory rejoices...and my flesh will dwell securely...not abandon my soul in Sheol"). This is detailing. Not only is He assured of resurrection of the body, He is also assured of the preservation of His soul, the safe return from Hell ("Sheol"). So, Christ Jesus would die, but He would not decay. Likewise, Christ was promised a safe

---

[238] Matthew 27:46
[239] Psalm 16:9–11

passage from Hell, and He was also shown the glory that He would assume upon His return: "Father, I want those you have given me to be with me where I am, and to see my glory, the glory you have given me because you loved me before the creation of the world."[240] This glory would be perfect – full of joy and pleasurable.

But Christ was not only shown His glory post-death, He was also shown the misery He would suffer: "Be not far from me, for trouble is near; For there is none to help. Many bulls have surrounded me; Strong bulls of Bashan have encircled me. They open wide their mouth at me, As a ravening and a roaring lion…"[241] He saw "bulls" and "lions" with no-one to help, not even God Himself: "Going a little farther, he fell with his face to the ground and prayed, 'My Father, if it is possible, may this cup be taken from me. Yet not as I will, but as you will.'"[242]

Why would He take all this trouble? Because of sin? Yes, and because of God's love for mankind: "For God so loved the world that he gave his one and only Son, that whoever believes in him shall not perish but have eternal life."[243] The wrath of God was unleashed upon God's own Son. This wrath is quenched when one believes

---

[240] John 17:24
[241] Psalm 22:11-13
[242] Matthew 26:39
[243] John 3:16

in Christ, but remains against all those who will not believe: "Whoever believes in the Son has eternal life; whoever does not obey the Son shall not see life, but the wrath of God remains on him."[244]

The Beauty of the Gospel

Here is, therefore, the simplicity and complexity of Grace: Mankind sins and must be punished. But God takes the form of a man and bears that punishment. Man walks free without a single lash on his back. God takes all the beating. This process is what we call salvation. It is beautiful as it is thought-provoking: "For it is by grace you have been saved through faith, and this not from yourselves; it is the gift of God."[245] What a gift!

We cannot understand the beauty of the Gospel until we understand Grace. Isaiah says: "How beautiful on the mountains are the feet of the messenger who brings good news, the good news of peace and salvation, the news that the God of Israel reigns!"[246]

There are three reasons why the Gospel is beautiful. First, it is beautiful because of its *content*. It is about freedom, and by no means condemnation: "Therefore, there is now no condemnation for those who are in

---

[244] John 3:36
[245] Ephesians 2:8
[246] Isaiah 52:7

Christ Jesus. For in Christ Jesus the law of the Spirit of Life has set you free from the law of sin and death."[247] It says to the dead, "You can live again." It says to the sinner, "You're now saved." It says to the prisoner, "You can now go free." It says to the dejected, "You can now be whole." It says to the wicked, "You're now right with God."

Isn't this the ministry that Jesus Christ announced He had come to do on earth? For He said, "The Spirit of the Lord is on me, because he has anointed me to proclaim good news to the poor. He has sent me to proclaim freedom for the prisoners and recovery of sight for the blind, to set the oppressed free."[248]

Second, the Gospel is beautiful because of its *counsel*. That those who believe in it will not perish but have everlasting life.[249] Even if they die the first time, they will not die the second time. They will only *sleep* in the Lord: "For we believe that Jesus died and rose again, and so we believe that God will bring with Jesus those who have fallen asleep in him."[250] Yes, those who have faith in Christ our Lord, only "sleep" and not die. They will be resurrected to be with the Lord forever. That is why the Gospel is beautiful.

---

[247] Romans 8: 1 and 2
[248] Luke 4:18
[249] See John 3:16
[250] 1 Thessalonians 4:14

And third, it is beautiful because of its *compliments*: "They replied, 'Believe in the Lord Jesus, and you will be saved--you and your household'"[251] And this is where Grace comes in. Simply believe. And you will be saved, including your loved ones. What can be more beautiful than that God has taken away sin, our fears, and our ultimate punishment – Hell – all because of simple faith in His finished work. That is Grace.

The discussed content, counsel and compliments of the Gospel have nothing to do with us. They all have everything to do with Christ Jesus our Lord. We are simply passive receivers. Christ has actively done all and everything. Our only duty is to believe, confess and accept: "If you confess with your mouth that Jesus is Lord and believe in your heart that God raised him from the dead, you will be saved."[252] Grace has given us an easy path. It demands our belief in the finished work of Jesus Christ, confessing it with our months and accepting it for our salvation. Grace does not want us to do rituals or sacrifices; it only requires us to exercise our faith in the finished work of Jesus Christ our Lord. That is just as simple as it gets.

Contrary to popular opinion, acceptance, believing and confessing ought not to form

---

[251] Acts 16:31
[252] Romans 10:9

the "ABC" formulaic of the Gospel. It must not be achieved via an altar call. It cannot be a tradition of "how people get saved." Indeed not. God is neither unreasonable nor an unjust judge who requires that all undergo a similar formulation. God does not only save people because they attended a church and answered an altar call. God, equally, does not condemn people because they failed to answer an altar call. This is human machination, human weakness, and perhaps a false confidence that, "We led people to the Lord."

God does not save people through a predictable patterned formula. God is sovereign; He cannot be contained in human tactics and innuendos. God has already saved people through the death of His Son, Jesus Christ, and now this manifestation differs from person to person, and it solely depends on God's own prerogative and providence.

Thus, a person can accept today, believe tomorrow, and confess the next day, and still be saved. Or a person can do all the three at the same time. Or it might take years or even decades for the person to completely confess what they believe or it can all happen in a split second. God is sovereign and it is His prerogative to save, no matter the circumstance or opportunity.

That is what makes it of Grace. Otherwise a preacher might think that they had everything to do with it. No. It has everything to do with God. A preacher is just a messenger. It is vital to contextualize Romans 10:14, "How then shall they call on him in whom they have not believed? and how shall they believe in him of whom they have not heard? and how shall they hear without a preacher?" Apostle Paul was trying to motivate the Roman Church to do evangelism. He was a minister to his own established church. It was important that they evangelized.

However, whether the Roman Church decided to evangelize or not, God would have found a preacher. Remember if people do not preach, God can use anything, including a donkey: "Then the LORD opened the donkey's mouth, and it said to Balaam, 'What have I done to you to make you beat me these three times?'"[253] The fact that God uses human agents to do His will is purely out of Grace. If God so desires, He can use anything, both to preach and to worship Him: "And do not think you can say to yourselves, 'We have Abraham as our father,' I tell you that out of these stones God can raise up children for Abraham."[254] That is what Apostle Paul advises, "And whatever you do, whether in word or deed, do it all in the name of the Lord Jesus, giving thanks to God the Father through

---

[253] Numbers 22:28
[254] Matthew 3:9

him."[255] Christ is everything. Whether you preach, sing, administer, lead or serve, give thanks to God. It is not because of you – it is because of Him!

Christ, is not, therefore, just the center of everything, He is everything. Through Him mankind's sins are forgiven and pardoned: "In whom we have redemption, the forgiveness of sins."[256] He instituted a new covenant by fulfilling the old, and He has adopted the role of the mediator of the new covenant: "Therefore, Christ is the mediator of a new covenant, so that those who are called may receive the promised eternal inheritance, now that He has died to redeem them from the transgressions committed under the first covenant."[257]

The Power of the Gospel – It's Free

The Gospel is only good news if its focus is on Grace. Any other preaching, however well-received, does not have the power to communicate Grace and save souls. It does not matter who preaches, if they preach a Gospel devoid of the message of Grace, that preacher is accursed: "But even if we or an angel from heaven should preach a gospel other than the one we preached to

---

[255] Colossians 3:17
[256] Colossians 1:14
[257] Hebrews 9:15

you, let them be under God's curse!"[258]

Paul addressed this issue against the Galatians: "I am astonished that you are so quickly deserting the one who called you by the grace of Christ and are turning to a different gospel."[259] There are different gospels out there. These gospels are fake, based on human innuendos and sophistication. They use the name of Christ in vain while glorifying and celebrating the achievement of men. These gospels tend to create a culture of two extremes. They may create a culture of "make me good and feel happy" syndrome. In this case, the preacher preaches to the ingratiation of people, to be approved among them. The preacher's objective is to make people like the preacher or commend the preacher. It is a gospel purely engrossed in psychology and human motivation. It is short-lived and has no eternal impact.

The other culture is hard on Grace. It victimizes the listener into fear and intimidation. People come out and confess their sins, not because of the love of God shown in the death of Christ, but because they are afraid to go to Hell or fear something bad will happen to them. The *Gospel of Fear* is not good news. It is logical and commonsensical, but it is not the reason why Christ died. Christ died because

---

[258] Galatians 1:8
[259] Galatians 1:6

of love. Hell was made for the devil and his angels: "Then he will say to those on his left, 'Depart from me, you who are cursed, into the eternal fire prepared for the devil and his angels.'"[260]

Christ came to reintroduce people back to the Father. He forgives people of their sins, no matter how terrible those sins are. He grants people pardon without conditions, except that they believe. His salvation is free: "Heal the sick, cleanse the lepers, raise the dead, cast out devils: freely ye have received, freely give."[261] The Gospel must be preached for free – because it is free. This is just as simple as it gets. There is no qualification or justification for *selling* the Gospel. Once it is sold, it, by its nature, becomes ineffective. It is called "Good News" because, in part, it is given and received for free. This rhymes well with the pith and ambit of Grace. Where the Gospel is exchanged for anything mortal or material, it becomes the work of human beings, and not of God. It ceases to be of Grace.

The Gospel was bequeathed to humanity in propitiation through Christ Jesus' death. No amount of money can buy the gifts of God: "Peter answered: 'May your money perish with you, because you thought you could buy the gift of God with

---

[260]Matthew 25:41
[261] Matthew 10:8

money!'"[262] Salvation cannot be attained through tricks. It is a work of generosity, of Grace. Jack L. Arnold illustrates:

> The basic meaning of propitiation is "appease" or "satisfy." What did the death of Christ appease or satisfy in the nature of God? In his very nature, God is holy and righteous. He can have no fellowship with anything that is sinful, including sinful men. Thus, God's wrath burns hot against sin and sinners because he must judge all sin. If he does not do this, he is not acting according to his perfect character. But, in love, God sent his Son Jesus Christ to be the perfect sacrifice for sin. No mere human being could have atoned for the sins of men because all are sinners. But Christ, who was a perfect human as well as truly divine, became the perfect sacrifice for sin. God poured out his wrath against sin on the person of Jesus Christ. Thus, the death of Christ appeased God's wrath and satisfied his holy, righteous demands against sin.[263]

---

[262] Acts 8:20
[263] Jack L. Arnold, "Propitiation: A Study on Romans 3:24-26," (http://reformedperspectives.org/newfiles/jac_arnold/NT.Arnold.Rom.19.html - retrieved: December 3rd, 2018)

The price of salvation could not be attained through human means. In other words, there was nothing of equal value to appease the wrath of God and provide for salvation. God must find something more equal or worthier than our humanity. It had, regrettably for God, and, fortunately for us, to be found in the "killing" of His own Son. Jesus Christ had to die to save humanity. God had to allow it although He loved His Son above anything else. Thus, it can be both improper and immoral to exchange the Gospel for monetary gains. Salvation has no equal value in money. Its value is measured in perfect blood. That blood only existed in God's Son – our Lord Jesus Christ.

The early Apostles preached the simple Gospel of Grace, and it bore tremendous results: "In the same way, the gospel is bearing fruit and growing throughout the whole world – just as it has been doing among you since the day you heard it and truly understood God's grace."[264] The gospel which grew and bore fruits, was the Gospel of Grace. It was understood to be of Grace, and nothing else. The preacher is not the focus of the Gospel, Christ is: "However, I consider my life worth nothing to me; my only aim is to finish the race and complete the task the Lord Jesus has given

---

[264] I Peter 4: 10; Colossians 1:6

me – the task of testifying to the good news of God's grace."[265]

Communicating Grace

God can choose anybody to communicate the message of Grace; it is not based on talent or class or prowess or privilege or education: "Although I am less than the least of all the Lord's people, this grace was given me: to preach to the Gentiles the boundless riches of Chris."[266] Success in the work of God cannot be attributed to any single individual; it is a work of cooperate-grace that God bestows upon members of His Body. The pastor cannot say that they are so powerful that they have grown the work of God. That is ignorance and arrogance. God's work is of Grace, and it may be accomplished through many workers: "By the grace God has given me, I laid a foundation as a wise builder, and someone else is building on it. But each one should build with care."[267]

Everything that is done in the name of the Lord is of Grace. We pray, preach, give and receive, perform rituals and sacraments, celebrate liturgies and minister to people through Grace. No-one should boast that they have this, accomplished that or

---

[265] Acts 20:24
[266] Hebrews 12:15; Ephesians 3:8
[267] II Cor. 9:8; I Corinthians 3:10

become who they are by themselves or because of themselves. We are who we are because of the Grace of God.

In Summary

By no means is the Gospel weak because it preaches Grace. It is because of Grace that the Gospel is powerful: "But it has now been revealed through the appearing of our Savior, Christ Jesus, who has destroyed death and has brought life and immortality to light through the gospel."[268]

And sometimes, the preaching of Grace may face opposition and attacks from the evil one, but it is only this Gospel which saves people and brings them before God the Father: "It is right for me to feel this way about all of you, since I have you in my heart and, whether I am in chains or defending and confirming the gospel, all of you share in God's grace with me."[269]

And to sum the two arguments, *vis*, that all who preach, should preach by His Grace, and that this same simple Grace has enormous power, here is what Paul says: "I became a servant of this gospel by the gift of God's grace given me through the working of his power."[270] Interestingly enough, you frequently hear preachers

---

[268] II Cor. 8:7; 2 Timothy 1:10
[269] Acts 11:23; Philippians 1:7
[270] Eph. 3:2; Ephesians 3:7

boasting about their abilities to persuade and dissuade their audiences.

No human being is capable of converting a soul. No amount of preaching or promulgation can move an iota on the scale of salvation. Every soul that was ever saved, did so by Grace through faith.

Eloquence, flamboyance or even oratorial buoyancy have no impact on the Gospel. Flashy speeches may greatly move the masses towards decisiveness or action – to vote for a candidate, buy a product or render a service – but they cannot change or transform a soul. When you see people getting saved or converted as a result of your preaching, it is testament to the power of His Grace working in a mortal vessel – you. And that is cause for praise and thanksgiving and not for boasting.

> Halleluiah, halleluiah, You have done it
> Not through force, but only by Your Spirit
> Taken all my pity, gory, pain and shame
> To cloth me in glory, pleasure and fame
> O Jesus, merciful, strong and Savior
> Let Your ways be my life and behavior.

7 | JEW AND GENTILE UNDER GRACE

Favor from Favoritism

Peter, a Jewish Apostle, is surprised when God sends him to the house of a non-Jew, Cornelius. From there Peter learns a new lesson: "Then Peter began to speak: 'I now truly understand that God does not show favoritism, but welcomes those from every nation who fear Him and do what is right. He has sent this message to the people of Israel, proclaiming the gospel of peace through Jesus Christ, who is Lord of all.…'"[271] He learns that Jesus Christ has become Lord of all – all peoples, Jews and Gentiles. The Bible agrees: "No! We believe it is through the grace of our Lord Jesus that we are saved, just as they are."[272]

In Chapter 6, we learned that the Gospel is a work of Grace. To be able to preach to people is not a matter of chance or coercion, it is one of Grace. The sinner is invited to receive a free gift of righteousness without paying any price that sin demands, death. Someone else, namely Christ, died on and for the sake of the sinner. It is Grace as well which

---

[271] Acts 10:34-36
[272] Acts 15:11

keeps Christ not returning early, giving the sinner an opportunity to repent: "The Lord is not slack concerning his promise, as some men count slackness; but is longsuffering to us-ward, not willing that any should perish, but that all should come to repentance."[273]

The Jews were elected by Grace. The non-Jews receive the Gospel also by Grace:

> Therefore no one will be declared righteous in God's sight by the works of the law; rather, through the law we become conscious of our sin. But now apart from the law the righteousness of God has been made known, to which the Law and the Prophets testify. This righteousness is given through faith in Jesus Christ to all who believe. There is no difference between Jew and Gentile, for all have sinned and fall short of the glory of God, and all are justified freely by his grace through the redemption that came by Christ Jesus.[274]

The act of Christ becoming a human being is one of Grace, apart from the fact that Christ Himself came full of Grace: "The Word became flesh and made his dwelling among us. We have seen his glory, the glory of the one and only Son, who came from the Father, full of grace and truth."[275] God's glory is now tied

---

[273] 2 Peter 3:9, see also footnote 105
[274] Romans 3:20-24
[275] John 1:14

to Grace. We have not seen any of God's glory until we first see His Grace. This becomes approachable glory, because in it God opens up a way to His throne.

All who became the Church's first apostles were chosen by Grace. Grace enabled them to be apostles and to advance the message of Grace throughout the world. God had purposed this long before the twelve apostles were chosen. It had been in God's divine plan that at some point in life, He would unleash His Grace to save humanity through the message of the prophets and apostles:

> Paul, a servant of Christ Jesus, called to be an apostle and set apart for the gospel of God — the gospel he promised beforehand through his prophets in the Holy Scripture regarding his Son, who as to his earthly life was a descendant of David, and who through the Spirit of holiness was appointed the Son of God in power by his resurrection from the dead: Jesus Christ our Lord. Through him we received grace and apostleship to call all the Gentiles to the obedience that comes from faith for his name's sake.[276]

This Grace continues to work wonderfully in those who are advancing the Gospel of Christ. It also worked wonderfully in Stephen: "Now

---

[276] Romans 1:1-5

Stephen, a man full of God's grace and power, performed great wonders and signs among the people."[277] Not only to the early Christians, but to everyone who believes in Christ, Grace has been apportioned: "But to each one of us grace has been given as Christ apportioned it."[278] And it continues to grow and even strengthen those who may be weary or even physically weak: "Do not be carried away by all kinds of strange teachings. It is good for our hearts to be strengthened by grace, not by eating ceremonial foods, which is of no benefit to those who do so."[279]

This basically translates into everything happening as a result of Grace, and the greatest of these is salvation itself. So, if anyone is saved by Grace, then it is because of God and not of that person's effort or goodness. God can take anyone and save them. They need not love God first and do something for God first. They are saved by God's gracious will: "For it is by grace you have been saved, through faith—and this is not from yourselves, it is the gift of God — not by works, so that no one can boast."[280]

Ten Ways in Which Grace Increases

It is important to note that Grace is, by

---

[277] Acts 6:8
[278] Ephesians 4:7
[279] Hebrews 13:9
[280] Ephesians 2:8-9

definition, not bequeathed on a few because they do or say or are of a certain disposition. That would not be Grace. Grace is already available to all – both Jews and Gentiles. However, some can neglect the Grace of God, while others can increase it in their own lives. The following are ways in which Grace may be strengthened in one's life:

First, through the knowledge of Christ: "Grace and peace be yours in abundance through the knowledge of God and of Jesus our Lord."[281] Moreover, Grace is made good when one becomes aware that they are no longer slaves of sin: "For sin shall no longer be your master, because you are not under the law, but under grace."[282]

Second, through God's presence: "Let us then approach God's throne of grace with confidence, so that we may receive mercy and find grace to help us in our time of need."[283] Being in God's presence, effectively, brings us the fullness of Christ, and thereby increases Grace because we spend time with Him who is full of Grace: "And of his fulness have all we received, and grace for grace."[284] In His presence, our spirits interact with Christ's, and we receive abundance of Grace: "The Lord Jesus Christ [be] with thy spirit. Grace [be] with you. Amen."[285]

---

[281] 2 Peter 1:2
[282] Romans 6:14
[283] Hebrews 4:16
[284] John 1:16
[285] 2 Timothy 4:22

Third, through service to others: "Each of you should use whatever gift you have received to serve others, as faithful stewards of God's grace in its various forms."[286] It is vital to qualify this verse, that it is not Grace to labor for others, but it is as a result of Grace that we labor for others. Any labor which is done in this way, will receive God's approval, and God will not forget it: "God is not unjust; he will not forget your work and the love you have shown him as you have helped his people and continue to help them."[287] The Bible accurately calls it, "The labor of love."

Fourth, through humility: "But he gives us more grace. That is why Scripture says: 'God opposes the proud but shows favor [grace] to the humble.'"[288]

Fifth, through giving: "But since you excel in everything—in faith, in speech, in knowledge, in complete earnestness and in the love we have kindled in you — see that you also excel in this grace of giving."[289] As argued elsewhere, God's new approach to giving is based on freedom, and not on persuasiveness: "Being justified freely by his grace through the redemption that is in Christ Jesus."[290]

Sixth, through receiving of God's salvation: "For the grace of God has appeared

---

[286] 1 Peter 4:10
[287] Hebrews 6:10
[288] James 4:6
[289] 2 Corinthians 8:7
[290] Romans 3:24

that offers salvation to all people."[291] And this is reinforced in Romans: "But God commendeth his love toward us, in that, while we were yet sinners, Christ died for us."[292]

Seventh, through weakness: "And he said unto me, My grace is sufficient for thee: for my strength is made perfect in weakness. Most gladly therefore will I rather glory in my infirmities, that the power of Christ may rest upon me."[293]

Eighth, through labor *with* God: "But by the grace of God I am what I am: and his grace which [was bestowed] upon me was not in vain; but I labored more abundantly than they all: yet not I, but the grace of God which was with me."[294] As Paul clarifies, this is not working for God first and then meriting His Grace. It is Grace first, and then, that Grace would bring strength, energy and willingness to do that which is God's work. As it is also written: "For it is God who works in you to will and to act in order to fulfill his good purpose,"[295] and "And if by grace, then [is it] no more of works: otherwise grace is no more grace. But if [it be] of works, then is it no more grace: otherwise work is no more work."[296]

Nineth, through decisiveness: "Thou therefore, my son, be strong in the grace that is

---

[291] Titus 2:11
[292] Romans 5:8
[293] 2 Corinthians 12:9
[294] 1 Corinthians 15:10
[295] Philippians 2:13
[296] Romans 11:6

in Christ Jesus."[297] This might look like an oxymoron, why the conjecture to be strong in Grace, should this not be natural to the recipient of Grace? The Lord has not taken our will power; He has only empowered us to use it well, to the glory of God. In the matters of decision, we play a key role in ensuring that we are continuing to believe in Him and to exercise His Grace. We also must be vigilant that Satan does not corrupt the Grace of God in our lives: "When anyone hears the message of the kingdom but does not understand it, the evil one comes and snatches away what was sown in his heart. This is the seed sown along the path."[298]

And tenth, through enterprise: "For you know the grace of our Lord Jesus Christ, that though he was rich, yet for your sake he became poor, so that you through his poverty might become rich."[299] Poverty is not a state of righteousness. Christ dealt with poverty in the same way He dealt with sin. He, graciously, became poor in order that we might become rich. In this passage and context, this is not spiritual richness; it is, in fact, material richness. The important thing to remember here is that Christ has already made material richness for us possible. It is our responsibility to be enterprising and to appropriate the bequeathed richness into profitability.

Christ discussed the power of shrewdness

---

[297] 2 Timothy 2:1
[298] Matthew 13:19
[299] 2 Corinthians 8:9

(defined here as sound judgment, and often resourcefulness, especially in practical matters). There is a difference between being shrewd and being a fraud: Fraud cheats; shrewdness just understands human nature. Human beings cannot be controlled, ruled or helped without a small dose of shrewdness; one needs a small amount of canniness to handle most human issues. Godly shrewdness is required in a world where most people we meet are tricksters, dishonest and frauds.

We cannot acquire property, succeed in business or achieve most promotions without some amount of shrewdness. And Christians to other Christians may act with zero shrewdness and still win, but no-one can win in money and property world with the people of this world without being shrewd, no matter who they are. Our Lord Jesus Christ taught us: "The master commended the dishonest manager because he had acted shrewdly. For the people of this world are shrewder in dealing with their own kind than are the people of the light."[300] In dealing with the people of this world in business or monetary things or in politics or academia, we have been given a dosage of Grace for that.

In Summary

The above noted, the most effective method of increasing in Grace is through the

---

[300] Luke 16:8

knowledge of God and Christ Jesus. Grace grows as we know God and Jesus better. From this knowledge, we also become partakers in God's divine nature and we experience many manifestations of Grace.

> O, the mysteries of this grace
> How unfathomable to a raw soul
> He who knew no sin, took my place
> What we have, He gave to us, all.

8 | FAVOR

Principle

In the Old Testament, God showed favor to certain individuals from time to time. Thus, a principle was set, even in pre-grace period, that God would, at some future time, show His unmerited favor to all. In Proverbs, we read, "He mocks proud mockers but shows favor to the humble and oppressed."[301] And this is what we saw repeated by James that, "God opposes the proud but shows favor to the humble."[302] This principle stands, regardless of the dispensation. It will always be that the humble will receive God's Grace, the proud will not.

In relation to New Testament understanding of Grace, this principle is not violated when Grace fails to extend to this category of people. Grace is still available to all, including the proud, except that, by its nature, pride will not bow to Grace. God, therefore, is vindicated when He punishes or opposes the proud, because they would not have none of His Grace.

Again in Proverbs, it is written, "One

---

[301] Proverbs 3:34
[302] James 4:6

who loves a pure heart and who speaks with grace will have the king for a friend."[303] Naturally, this is the norm. But when God decided to love the sinner, and extended His Grace to mankind despite their rejection of Him, this was a game-changer.

Two passages in the Old Testament provide a cogent attestation to God's desire to give Grace. In Zechariah, it is written: "So I shepherded the flock marked for slaughter, particularly the oppressed of the flock. Then I took two staffs and called one Favor and the other Union, and I shepherded the flock,"[304] and further, "Then I took my staff called Favor and broke it, revoking the covenant I had made with all the nations."[305] Surely, God has now made a permanent covenant of love, based purely on Grace.

Isaiah is an interesting prophet. God had shown him what Grace would look like in dispensations to come. God had revealed that Grace would be extended to the sinner, and Isaiah protested: "But when grace is shown to the wicked, they do not learn righteousness; even in a land of uprightness they go on doing evil and do not regard the majesty of the LORD."[306] Isaiah could not believe that people who did not deserve it, the wicked, would receive Grace. This

---

[303] Proverbs 22:11
[304] Zechariah 11:7
[305] Zechariah 11:10
[306] Isaiah 26:10

would be amazing Grace.

As indicated, in the Old Testament, there was nothing close to Grace as we know it in this dispensation.

Prototypical Factor

Even in the Old Testament, through action or statement, God would indicate what He had in mind for the future. The glorious Grace bequeathed to mankind through Christ whereby without man's active will or act, God simply chooses to forgive, save and bless them, was shown in flashes. For example, in Ezra, we read, "But now, for a brief moment, the LORD our God has been gracious in leaving us a remnant and giving us a firm place in his sanctuary, and so our God gives light to our eyes and a little relief in our bondage."[307] However, even here, the imagery is tantalizing. It was "for a brief moment" and just "a little relief" in their difficulty times.

Another example is illustrated in and through the life and calling of Moses. Moses acknowledges, "Moses said to the LORD, 'You have been telling me, lead these people, but you have not let me know whom you will send with me. You have said, 'I know you by name and you have found favor with me.'"[308] Moses did not do

---

[307] Ezra 9:8
[308] Exodus 33:12-14

anything to merit God's favor, God simply chose him, even from birth. Then, even when Moses blundered, murdered an Egyptian and fled from responsibility, God still pursued him and brought him to accomplish the task for which He had called him. This was Grace, and a slew of others like David, Joseph, Mary the mother of Jesus, and so on, had experienced these flashes. But complete fullness of God's Grace came with Christ Jesus.

In Samuel, we see a type of God-humanity relationship that is a clear depiction of the Grace dispensation as we now know it: "But David took an oath and said, 'Your father knows very well that I have found favor in your eyes, and he has said to himself – Jonathan must not know this or he will be grieved.' Yet as surely as the LORD lives and as you live, there is only a step between me and death."[309] David and Jonathan, Saul's son, had a relationship that is a quintessence of divine Grace. Jonathan would have, and indeed, did give up his own life for that of David. He did this even at the expense of his own relationship with his father, the king. This was a prototype of the real Grace to come.

However, the majority of the favor in the Old Testament is based on what could be referred to as "Conditional" and "Reiteratory" favor. The former is based on

---

[309] 1 Samuel 20:3

a condition that must be fulfilled in future, and the latter is based on a past performance or past act of favor.

Conditional Factor

God promised to do something or did something in the then present for certain people. And those people would peg their request or agenda on that encounter with God. The essence was to be rewarded in some form in the future or in the moment. In Numbers, we read, "'If we have found favor in your eyes,' they said, 'let this land be given to your servants as our possession. Do not make us cross the Jordan.'"[310] Favor was the precondition for certain actions to be done in the future. This is the same pith of Samuel, "Then David said to Achish, 'If I have found favor in your eyes, let a place be assigned to me in one of the country towns, that I may live there. Why should your servant live in the royal city with you?'"[311]

Shechem said to Dinah's father and brothers, "Let me find favor in your eyes, and I will give you whatever you ask."[312] And "The people who survive the sword will find favor in the wilderness; I will come

---

[310] Numbers 32:5
[311] 1 Samuel 27:5
[312] Genesis 34:11

to give rest to Israel."[313] In these verses, a promise of favor is tied to a future condition. Similarly, when Jacob [Israel] was nearing his death, he asked Joseph for a future favor: "When the time drew near for Israel to die, he called for his son Joseph and said to him, 'If I have found favor in your eyes, put your hand under my thigh and promise that you will show me kindness and faithfulness. Do not bury me in Egypt.'"[314] A special type of favor Hannah referred to is neither due to present nor future reward, but the context favors a future reward, "'May your servant find favor in your eyes.' Then she went her way and ate something, and her face was no longer downcast."[315] Of course, we know that Prophet Samuel was the reward of this event.

A quintessential conditional future or present favor is found in Judges, "Gideon replied, 'If now I have found favor in your eyes, give me a sign that it is really you talking to me.'"[316]

What we read in Psalms, "For the LORD God is a sun and shield; the LORD bestows favor and honor; no good thing does he withhold from those whose walk is blameless,"[317] is both a principle and a

---

[313] Jeremiah 31:2
[314] Genesis 47:29
[315] 1 Samuel 1:18, NIV
[316] Judges 6:17
[317] Psalms 84:11

condition. A principle is established in "the LORD bestows favor and honor" and the condition is in "no good thing does he withhold from those whose walk is blameless." And throughout the Old Testament, God bestowed favor on those who walked blameless, and this is what we shall explore in the ensuing section.

Reiteratory Factor

In Genesis, we read that, "But Noah found favor in the eyes of the LORD."[318] God destroyed the known world with water but Noah was spared. Noah was spared because he walked blamelessly. Noah was spared because of a past act or behavior. This was favor because of, not in spite of.

Let us look at some examples. In Samuel, it is written, "Then the king said to Ziba, 'All that belonged to Mephibosheth is now yours.' 'I humbly bow,' Ziba said. 'May I find favor in your eyes, my lord the king.'"[319] As noted, David and Jonathan had a great personal friendship and David was simply, naturally, doing Jonathan a favor. David was honoring his friend's son, Mephibosheth.

Another example is illustrated in the life of Jacob and Esau, his brother. In Genesis, we read, "I have cattle and donkeys, sheep

---

[318] Genesis 6:8
[319] 2 Samuel 16:4

and goats, male and female servants. Now I am sending this message to my lord, that I may find favor in your eyes."[320] Jacob is explicit that he needs to pacify his brother through a bribe. And Esau responds, "Esau asked, 'What do you mean by all these flocks and herds I met?' 'To find favor in your eyes, my lord,' he said."[321] The conversation proceeds, "'No, please!' said Jacob. 'If I have found favor in your eyes, accept this gift from me. For to see your face is like seeing the face of God, now that you have received me favorably.'"[322] And Esau and Jacob again converse, "Esau said, 'Then let me leave some of my men with you.' 'But why do that?' Jacob asked. 'Just let me find favor in the eyes of my lord.'"[323] This shows favor requested and granted because of a past misdeed.

A general understanding of favor is also contained in this situation: "You have saved our lives," they said. "May we find favor in the eyes of our Lord; we will be in bondage to Pharaoh."[324] And when one is granted a request, they have naturally found favor: "Joab fell with his face to the ground to pay him honor, and he blessed the king. Joab said, 'Today your servant knows that he has found favor in your eyes, my lord the king,

---

[320] Genesis 32:5
[321] Genesis 33:8
[322] Genesis 33:10
[323] Genesis 33:15
[324] Genesis 47:25

because the king has granted his servant's request."[325]

And, of course, attractiveness is a classic example of how people find favor one with another. It was so with Esther: "Now the king was attracted to Esther more than to any of the other women, and she won his favor and approval more than any of the other virgins. So, he set a royal crown on her head and made her queen instead of Vashti."[326]

Joseph had a series of misfortunes, but also of favors with people. In Genesis 39, Joseph found favor with Potiphar: "Joseph found favor in his eyes and became his attendant. Potiphar put him in charge of his household, and he entrusted to his care everything he owned."[327] And this would lead to finding favor with Pharaoh himself: "When the days of mourning had passed, Joseph said to Pharaoh's court, 'If I have found favor in your eyes, speak to Pharaoh for me. Tell him.'"[328]

Lot appreciated the angels who had spared his life: "Your servant has found favor in your eyes, and you have shown great kindness to me in sparing my life."[329] This is because of what Abraham did which had been vicariously carried forward to Lot.

---

[325] 2 Samuel 14:22
[326] Esther 2:17
[327] Genesis 39:4
[328] Genesis 50:4
[329] Genesis 19:19

God spared Lot's life because of Abraham, Lot's uncle.

Beauty

Other times in the Old Testament, favor depicts beauty. This is what we see in Proverbs, "She will give you a garland to grace your head and present you with a glorious crown,"[330] and again, "They will be life for you, an ornament to grace your neck."[331]

In Psalms, we read, "You are the most excellent of men and your lips have been anointed with grace, since God has blessed you forever."[332] These, and equally-situated scenarios of favor show the esthetics use of the word favor and are repeated several times in the Psalms.

Ten Characteristics of a Blessing from God

There is human favor, and then there is divine favor (or Grace). Divine favor is also called God's blessings. Because God has had mercy and shown us Grace, He has also in the same act bequeathed to us blessings. "Blessings" from human beings only grant human favor. Human favor is short-lived, based on stimulus and

---

[330] Proverbs 4:9
[331] Proverbs 3:22
[332] Psalms 45:2

response, is limited, and creates a sense of entitlement. Human blessings are vindictive and they do create in the possessor avarice and boastfulness. They have no eternal value,[333] they are self-centered and they die with the possessor.[334]

However, God's true favor is a true blessing because:

First, it adds no sorrow to it, "The blessing of the LORD, it maketh rich, and he addeth no sorrow with it.";[335] "And at the end of ten days, their appearance was better and healthier than all the young men who were eating the king's food."[336]

Second, it does not fill one with pride or boastfulness, "For it is by grace you have been saved through faith, and this not from yourselves; it is the gift of God, not by works, so that no one can boast. For we are God's workmanship, created in Christ Jesus to do good works, which God prepared in advance as our way of life;"[337] "He has saved us and called us with a holy calling, not because of our own works, but by His own purpose and by the grace He granted us in Christ Jesus before time eternal;"[338]

---

[333] See Matthew 6:19-21
[334] Luke 12:20-21
[335] Proverbs 10:22, KJV
[336] Daniel 1:15
[337] Ephesians 2:8-10
[338] 2 Timothy 1:9

and "For we maintain that a man is justified by faith apart from works of the law."[339]

Third, it did not come because of works, but because of Grace. It is a gift, "The LORD has greatly blessed my master, and he has become rich. He has given him sheep and cattle, silver and gold, menservants and maidservants, and camels and donkeys."[340]

Fourth, it leads to holiness, "Indeed, every pot in Jerusalem and Judah will be holy to the LORD of Hosts, and all who sacrifice will come and take some pots and cook in them. And on that day there will no longer be a Canaanite in the house of the LORD of Hosts."[341]

Fifth, it glorifies God, "So whether you eat or drink or whatever you do, do it all for the glory of God;"[342] "And whatever you do, in word or deed, do it all in the name of the Lord Jesus, giving thanks to God the Father through Him;"[343] "If anyone speaks, he should speak as one conveying the words of God. If anyone serves, he should serve with the strength God provides, so that in all things God may be glorified through Jesus Christ, to whom be the glory and the power forever and ever. Amen;"[344]

---

[339] Romans 3:28
[340] Genesis 24:35
[341] Zechariah 14:21
[342] 1 Corinthians 10:31
[343] Colossians 3:17
[344] 1 Peter 4:11

and "Amen! Praise and glory and wisdom and thanks and honor and power and strength be to our God for ever and ever. Amen!"[345]

Sixth, it is duly received with thanksgiving or gratitude, "For everything God created is good, and nothing is to be rejected if it is received with thanksgiving;"[346] "He who observes a special day does so to the Lord; he who eats does so to the Lord, for he gives thanks to God; and he who abstains does so to the Lord and gives thanks to God;"[347] "The earth is the Lord's, and the fullness thereof;"[348] "If I partake in the meal with thankfulness, why am I denounced because of that for which I give thanks?;"[349] and "They will prohibit marriage and require abstinence from certain foods that God has created to be received with thanksgiving by those who *believe and know the truth*."[350]

Seventh, it makes rich without toil, "The blessing of the LORD brings wealth, without painful toil for it."[351]

Eighth, it grows irrespective of conditions, "Now Isaac sowed seed in the land, and in that very year he reaped a

---

[345] Revelation 7:12
[346] 1 Timothy 4:4
[347] Romans 14:6
[348] 1 Corinthians 10:26
[349] 1 Corinthians 10:30
[350] 1 Timothy 4:3 (emphasis added)
[351] Proverbs 10:22

hundredfold. And the LORD blessed him."[352]

Nineth, it gives one the power to become wealthy, "But remember that it is the LORD your God who gives you the power to gain wealth, in order to confirm His covenant that He swore to your fathers, as it is this day."[353]

And tenth, it comes in abundance and may not end, "Amaziah asked the man of God, 'What should I do about the hundred talents I have given to the army of Israel?' And the man of God replied, 'The LORD is able to give you much more than this,'"[354] and "The steadfast love of the Lord never ceases, his mercies never come to an end; they are new every morning; great is your faithfulness."[355] It is Grace when any of the two happens: You invest nothing and you gain everything. Or you invest very little and you harvest in abundance.

In Summary

God has always shown favor. Generally, in creating all humans, God has favored and blessed us all. However, and specifically, God chose, blessed and favored certain people (such as the Israelites) up and above

---

[352] Genesis 26:12
[353] Deuteronomy 8:18
[354] 2 Chronicles 25:9; Proverbs 8:21
[355] Lamentations 3:22-23

the general favor He has for all of His creation.

But in the New Testament, under Grace, God's unmerited favor is available to all – irrespective of nationality, ancestry, religion or any characteristic. It has been God's desire from the beginning to bless and favor His people. "In Christ," He has fulfilled that desire. The only qualification for appropriating God's favor is, "Whoever believes in Jesus Christ."

> I am loved, indeed, I am
> I am loved by the Great I AM
> No waters can drown this love
> For its been reserved for me above.

9 | GRACE AND TITHING

Tithing in Pre-Law Period

Tithe was before the Law of Moses was given. But the context is very important. Tithe was given after the blessing, not before: "Then Melchizedek king of Salem brought out bread and wine; he was the priest of God Most High. And he blessed him and said: 'Blessed be Abram of God Most High, Possessor of Heaven and earth; And blessed be God Most High, who has delivered your enemies into your hand.' And he gave him a tithe of all."[356] Abram is not commanded to tithe pre-law; he does so out of his abundance, out of grace. God never commanded Abram to tithe; Abram did it simply because he wanted to.

Jacob, Abraham's grandson gave a tithe. Then Jacob made a vow, saying, "If God will be with me and will keep me on this journey that I take, and will give me food to eat and garments to wear, and I return to my father's house in safety, then the LORD will be my God. This stone, which I have set up as a pillar, will be God's house, and of all that You give me I will surely give a

---

[356] Genesis 14:18-20

tenth to You."[357] In this situation, Jacob gave a tithe as a form of a guarantee, even a form of bribe, to God. His own sense of insecurity caused him to seek God's help in this endeavor. Of course, this is not to undermine the veracity of tithing; it is, rather, to show that tithing was used in this way at times, as a form of seeking God's guaranteed help in difficult times.

Tithing during the Law Period

> Thus, all the tithe of the land, of the seed of the **land** or of the fruit of the **tree**, is the LORD'S; it is holy to the LORD. If, therefore, a man wishes to redeem part of his tithe, he shall add to it one-fifth of it. For every tenth part of **herd or flock**, *whatever passes under the rod, the tenth one shall be holy to the LORD. He is not to be concerned whether it is good or bad, nor shall he exchange it; or if he does exchange it, then both it and its substitute shall become holy. It shall not be redeemed.* These are the commandments which the LORD commanded Moses *for the sons of Israel* at Mount Sinai.[358]

Strictly speaking, tithing was a

---

[357] Gen. 28:20–22
[358] Leviticus 27: 31-34, (emphasis added)

comprehensive Jewish regime. It starts here with the land – it's the LORD's and a tenth of it was to be given to the LORD. Then the tree, and the herd and the flock – the tenth of each belonged to the LORD. If, by extension, this rule was to be followed today, basically, everything we own would warrant a tenth part to be dedicated to the Lord, not only a tenth of our moneys. Or we would have to sell all we possess and give a tenth to the Lord.

It is vital to observe the principle underlying tithing: "…whatever passes under the rod, the tenth one shall be holy to the LORD. He is not to be concerned whether it is good or bad, nor shall he exchange it; or if he does exchange it, then both it and its substitute shall become holy. It shall not be redeemed." God was prepared to receive any tenth part, no matter how good or bad it was. It was a form of gamble or risk-taking undertaking. Sometimes God got the best, and sometimes the worst. This was also true of the people.

Moreover, tithing was compulsory to the people of Israel – for the sons of Israel. It was a requirement of everyone, including the Levites who gave a form of tithe of tithe. A distinction is to be made between Judaism and Christianity: The former was a national religion while the latter is mostly a personal relationship. Being in a national religion, the Israelites were mandated to obey all the statutes God set forth before them. This also included tithing as prescribed. Because of its national character, administration of the tithing regime was institutionalized, too. Thus, the Levites were some aspect of appointed authorities (internal revenue agents) who received and managed the tithe on behalf of God.

Further, owing to its national character, the element of willingness or willful offering was eliminated. People were compelled to tithe. For example, when some people did not take the tithe to God, God indicted the whole nation: "You are under a curse--your whole nation because you are robbing me."[359] It seems, from this indictment, that it was not up to an individual; it was compulsory to tithe. The repercussions of failure to tithe were national in consequence. The "sin" of one person could affect the entire nation. It was, therefore, necessary that there was a form of national management of the tithing regime:

> Then the LORD said to Aaron, 'You shall have no inheritance in their land nor own any portion among them; *I am your portion and your inheritance among the sons of Israel.*' To the sons of Levi, behold, I have given all the tithe in Israel

---

[359] Malachi 3:9

> for an inheritance, in return for their service which they perform, the service of the tent of meeting. The sons of Israel shall not come near the tent of meeting again, or they will bear sin and die. Only the Levites shall perform the service of the tent of meeting, and they shall bear their iniquity; it shall be a perpetual statute throughout your generations, and among the sons of Israel they shall have no inheritance. For the tithe of the sons of Israel, which they offer as an offering to the LORD, I have given to the Levites for an inheritance; therefore, I have said concerning them, 'They shall have no inheritance among the sons of Israel.[360]

Aaron was the temporal High Priest (*Kohen Gadol*). He was forbidden or precluded from having any earthly inheritance; God was his portion: "I am your portion and your inheritance among the sons of Israel." Aaron was entitled to receiving a tithe. He was to be dedicated (to be holy) to the service of the tabernacle. Levites are the descendants of Levi, one of the twelve tribes of Israel (Jacob). The *Kohens* (priests) are also descended from Levi. Both are integrated in Jewish and Samaritan societies, but they keep their distinctive statuses. The

---

[360] Number 18: 20-24

Kohens, who are the descendants of Aaron, were designated as the priestly class (the *Kohanim*).

To better understand this concept, a quote is made from the New Living Translation, "As for the tribe of Levi, your relatives, I will compensate them for their service in the tabernacle. *Instead of an allotment of land*, I will give them the tithes from the entire land of Israel," (verse 21 above). The Levites received a tithe on behalf of God, for "their service in the tabernacle."

The Levites were set apart (to be holy) for the work of the tabernacle. The tabernacle was an elaborate sacrificial tent of very detailed processes and procedures. It was divided into three compartments: The Outer Court, the Holy Place and the Holy of Holies (the Holiest). Their work in the Outer Court, the Holy Place and the Holy of Holies, with every brazen, silvery and golden emblems, respectively, were so elaborate that doing any other work, in addition, would have been impossible. God's wisdom assigned them a portion from all the produce of the land to be theirs.[361] They were not directly entitled to

---

[361] After Joshua captured the Promised Land (or Canaan), he distributed the land among the children of Jacob (Israel) with the exception of Levi. That meant that the land was to be shared among only 11 tribes. But Israel had 12 children (tribes), so God through Joshua cropped the two sons of Joseph

the land – to till it and cultivate crops and keep animals. They would benefit from other people's work on land, trees and fields. That way, they would concentrate on the work of God in the tabernacle.

The Levites themselves,[362] had to give a tenth of the tithes they received as an offering to the Lord: "Speak to the Levites and say to them: 'When you receive from the Israelites the tithe I give you as your inheritance, you must present a tenth of that tithe as the LORD's offering.'"[363]

The tithe was just one form of the offerings that were available to the Israelites: "But you shall seek the LORD at the place which the LORD your God will choose from all your tribes, to establish His name there for His dwelling, and there you shall come. There you shall bring your burnt offerings, your sacrifices, your tithes, the contribution of your hand, your votive [ritualistic or ceremonial] offerings, your freewill offerings, and the firstborn of your

---

(Ephraim and Manasseh) into the lineage, and thus, restoring the tribes of Israel to 12. Levi would depend on the tithes collected from the land of the 12 to survive. See the story in the Book of Joshua 13 to 22.

[362] See the change of roles in the New Testament in Acts 4: 36-37, "Joseph, a Levite from Cyprus, whom the apostles called Barnabas (meaning Son of Encouragement), sold a field he owned, brought the money, and laid it at the apostles' feet."

[363] Numbers 18:26

herd and of your flock."[364]

Tithe or ten percent of the crops was to be set aside each year: "People of Israel, every year you must set aside ten percent of your grain harvest."[365] There were tithing festivals every year in Israel. The festivals were quintessentially meant for the Israelites. For example, "You shall not eat anything which dies of itself. You may give it to the alien who is in your town, so that he may eat it, or you may sell it to a foreigner, for you are a holy people to the LORD your God," (verse 21). These festivals and rules were meant for the Israelites, not foreigners or pagans or aliens. And the rationale was to set apart a remnant of God's people who were committed to obeying God always. These, then, would serve as a sample of how God desired His people to be and behave – to be holy.

These ceremonial rules were many and intricate. The purpose was stated in Deuteronomy: "You shall eat in the presence of the LORD your God, at the place where He chooses to establish His name, the tithe of your grain, your new wine, your oil, and the firstborn of your herd and your flock, *so that you may learn to fear the LORD your God always,*" (verse 23, emphasis added).

---

[364] Deuteronomy 12:5-6
[365] Deuteronomy 14:22, (CEV)

As noted, God formally instituted tithing under the Law of Moses. Before the Law, people had a choice. Tithing was an act of personal will, and was not institutional. But it became formal and institutionalized during the Law Period.

It was offered to the priests to support the priests and the Levites. When it was abused, God, through Prophet Malachi, laid out the dual blessings attached to tithing under Law:

> 'Bring all the tithes into the storehouse, that there may be food in My house, and try Me now in this,' Says the Lord of hosts, 'If I will not open for you the windows of heaven and pour out for you such blessing that there will not be room enough to receive it. And I will rebuke the devourer for your sakes, so that he will not destroy the fruit of your ground, nor shall the vine fail to bear fruit for you in the field,' Says the Lord of hosts.[366]

The principle here was obedience, and not tithing; it was actions and not the resources. First, God had already stated that He could "pour out for you such blessing that there will not be room enough to receive it." God had and has abundance of resources. It is

---

[366] Malachi 3:10-11

not because He did not have resources that He wanted to receive a tithe.

Second, God does prevent and protect already available resources from being wasted, "I will rebuke the devourer for your sakes, so that he will not destroy the fruit of your ground, nor shall the vine fail to bear fruit for you in the field."

And third, "blessings" in the Old Covenant context, had a connotation of material prosperity. Blessings meant food, crops, animals and fruitfulness in the womb.

However, the Old Covenant blessings were conditional blessings. God, who had and has in abundance of everything, first tested His people to obey Him before He could release extra blessings into their lives. It is important to note here that, this principle seemed to have been efficacious only to extra blessings as opposed to basic blessings. For hitherto, God, even in Old Covenant time, had allowed His sun to shine upon both those who obeyed Him and those who did not. He had given rain to both the legally righteous people and those who were not righteous by the standards of the Law.

God already blessed His people in terms of basic blessings. He provided for all their basic needs. He created everything they enjoyed under the sun. But in Malachi, He was testing their obedience. If they obeyed Him, vis-à-vis the act of tithing, He would release the blessings upon them. Just like any act of obedience unlocks the "windows of Heaven," so was the requirement under the Law when obedience to tithing was done. To reiterate this rule, God reminded those Malachi spoke to that He did not change: "I the LORD, do not change."[367] The Lord's principles are unchanging. But it is important to note that tithing was a command and demanded obedience. It was a prescription of the Law.

God, at the time of Malachi, dealt with an agrarian society. Their occupations were usually subsistence farming. And God dealt with them as their situation demanded. Although it is usual to equate this command to tithing in monetary terms, it was measured at that time in agricultural terms. The store-house was the place of worship, and tithing was to support and maintain the work of the Levites and priests. God instituted this practice to sustain His work in the tent of meeting. The Levites and priests did not have any other regular jobs where they could receive an income, and in His generosity, God provided a way of sustenance through the tithe.

Would God rebuke the devourer of the crops of the Israelite people who obeyed the Lord's commands, especially the command to tithe? Of course, He would. But He would no less rebuke the thief who

---

[367] Malachi 3:6a

wanted to attack any of His people who was obedient to Him than He would for a tither. The principle is the same. Under the Law, God promised He would rebuke the devourer on behalf of those who tithed to keep their produce from being destroyed.

It is very important to note that it is not God who is the devourer; He merely rebukes the devourer. The enemy, and by extension, the devil, is always prowling around to find someone to attack.[368] The enemy will attack anything, including the produce of crops and animals unless the Lord protects them: "Unless the LORD builds the house, the builders labor in vain. Unless the LORD watches over the city, the guards stand watch in vain."[369]

Old Testament "blessings" were limited in scope; they seemed to have only covered earthly things.[370] They were provided in terms of material possessions – grain, wine, land, crops, meat, milk, fruit, and etc. They were stored on earth in granaries and flocks. They were vulnerable to the enemy – they could wither, die, be stolen or perish. The enemy had access to them. The people of Israel had to depend on God's protection to guard crops, animals, and etc.

Classes of Tithing

---

[368] See 1 Peter 5:8; John 10:10
[369] Psalm 127:1
[370] See "Ten Characteristics of a Blessing" on p. 105

The first hint of tithing in the Bible happens in the pre-law, Patriarchal Period, "Then Melchizedek king of Salem brought out bread and wine. He was priest of God Most High, and he blessed Abram, saying, 'Blessed be Abram by God Most High, Creator of Heaven and earth. And praise be to God Most High, who delivered your enemies into your hand.' Then Abram gave him a *tenth of everything*."[371] These verses seem to suggest that there were more than one class of tithes – "tenth of everything." This would mean tithing was not only limited to crops and animals.

This concept is similarly repeated in the pre-law period with Jacob, with a caveat, "…And *of all that you give me* I will give a full tenth to you."[372] In both of these incidents, tithe was promised or was given by the lesser to the greater, before the lesser had a name-change encounter with God, and it was given or to be given on "everything" or in "all that you give me." Similarly, in both cases, the giver *willingly* gave or promised to give. It can be argued and concluded that tithe was not a duty but a mixture of grace (gratitude and love) and personal commitment in the pre-law period.

Under the Mosaic Law, tithe became a duty and obligation. Tithe was mandatory

---

[371] Genesis 14:18–20 (emphasis added)
[372] Genesis 28:22, (emphasis added)

to the Israelites. Tithe took on the following characteristics:

- It became a system;
- It became organized in a seven-year cycle;
- The first tithe was one tenth of agricultural produce and was given to the Levites every year. This was to be consumed *within* the tabernacle;
- The second tithe took place on year one, that was to be brought to the place of the meeting.

No Tithing in New Testament

In the Old Covenant, tithing was required. However, there is no evidence in the Bible that tithing is a New Testament phenomenon. It is no longer the case for believers in Christ to abide by the old ceremonial festivals of tithing, and so on. Believers are set free from such observances. No-one is punished in the New Testament for not tithing. It is heretic and diminishing to God's redemptive plan to hook people to ideas that unless they tithe, God would not bless them. It is equally erroneous to preach that additional blessings come from acts of tithing. Tithing is not only from finances, it's from all that people owned; and if that was the case, by

Malachi standards, we would all be unredeemed, robbers and thieves. God does not need us to tithe to act on our behalf and prohibit the devourer from wasting away our finances.

Someone wrote: "You absolutely do not have to tithe. God will still love you just as much whether you tithe or not. But now that you know the benefits God promises if you do tithe, why would you not want to enjoy those extra blessings?"[373] This, too, is purely a half truth. Indeed, God simply loves us, whether we tithe or not. In fact, under the New Covenant, there is no requirement to tithing. Giving is purely an act of Grace and is demonstrated by willingness and according as someone has purposed in their hearts. There is no number, no percentage.

People have gone to lengths to prescribe ways, methodologies and strategies in tithing. The following is one of the good examples – philosophically correct, but spiritually invalid:

> Sometimes the math is scary – especially when you're going through a financial hardship. But the Lord calls us to have faith. The beauty about 10% is that the amount you give adjusts with your income. But as Christians, we want to give more than that when

---

[373] Author unknown

> we're able. That's why you should follow the Three Phases of Giving. During the Foundation Phase of the Three Phases of Wealth, give 10% to your church. As you advance through the Three Phases of Wealth, you'll advance through the Three Phases of Giving. This approach helps you determine how much you should be giving beyond your tithe. You should tithe during hardships. The Lord will pull you through. And when he blesses you, you'll be able to give back even more.[374]

This so-called, "Truth in Financial Planning," moves from ten percent income donation to giving one's tithe to charities and ministries. And finally, it proposes leaving behind one's estate to a Christian organization or ministry upon their demise.

Sounds very sound, doesn't it? This is all unbiblical, and anyone reading this who is unschooled into the intricacies of biblical theology might think that they have stumbled upon valid New Testament teaching. This teaching would not even measure up to the standard of the obsolete Old Testament, let alone to the rigor of Grace. The fact that someone mentions ten

---

[374] Michael Gauthier, "Should You Really Tithe During Hardships?" <https://truthinfinancialplanning.com/tithing-during-hardships/> April 3rd, 2014

percent in the same sentence as tithe does not make it biblically valid. The allusion to faith does not justify heresy, either.

In fact, most ardent supporters of the New Testament tithe would pour scorn on this treatise and shun it as heretic. Those who depend on tithe as the main source of revenue may even proscribe their members from reading this book. But even doing so will not right a wrong or legitimatize tithing as divinely mandated under Grace.

Many groups so-called prosperity ministries have enriched themselves at the expense of their deceived masses. Usually, it is only the Minister or preacher who gets "blessed" while the followers continue struggling financially or materially. These ministries have duped people and nations under dubiously questionable deductions from Malachi[375] and Proverbs: "Honor the LORD with your wealth, with the first fruits of all your crops."[376] The Malachi order preaches obedience. At the time, Israel was required to obey God by tithing. If they did, they were blessed, and if they did not, they came under a curse. The Proverb 3:9 order focuses on honor – and this included giving a portion of one's increase in crops or produce, which was then, a measure of wealth or one's livelihood.

---

[375] See Malachi 3:8-10
[376] Proverbs 3:9

The New Testament has refined the concepts of obedience and honor. First, we have all obeyed God through Jesus Christ. Or else, our so-called obedience or righteousness is as filthy rags.[377] Whoever believes in Jesus Christ has obeyed the entire Scripture and is saved. That is the only way for it to be of Grace.

And second, we honor God by accepting and believing in His begotten Son. We do this by Grace through faith.

There is no-one who can argue against the fact that financial resources are required to manage churches and Christian organizations. A "tithe" or any such similarly-situated offering may be prescribed as a matter of canon or church regulations. In that case, a church or ministry should inform its adherents that tithes are collected for the purposes of church administration. The finances may not be collected as a fulfilment of divine or moral obligation. That ended with the appearing of Grace.

To justify tithing in the New Testament or under Grace, most church congregations reference Leviticus, "And all the tithes of the land, whether of the seed of the land or of the fruit of the tree, is the LORD's. It is holy to the LORD."[378] And then they interpret this verse as suggesting that all that

---

[377] Isaiah 64:6
[378] Leviticus 27:30

we own, including our income, belongs to the Lord. There is an insinuation that those who do not tithe in the Church Era are wrong or mistaken or sinning. This is not true.

The verse referenced above is a statement of fact. It is true that all the land, in fact, all creation, belongs to God. That is the basis of the Creationist Theory – God made all things. It is equally true that all of the things God made, are holy – or set apart for Him. But He has given them all to us for our enjoyment: "Command those who are rich in this present world not to be arrogant nor to put their hope in wealth, which is so uncertain, but to put their hope in God, who richly provides us with everything for our enjoyment."[379] This is the new way God deals with us; He gives us everything, freely, unconditionally, for our enjoyment. And this is for everyone – for sinners as well as for saints.[380]

In the Law Period and the Old Covenant in general, God's material blessings to people were not gifts; they were conditional offers: "Honor the LORD with your wealth and with the first fruits of all your harvest; *then* your barns will be filled with plenty, and your vats will overflow with new wine."[381] This does not establish the institution of tithe or *ma'aser* (Hebrew)

---

[379] 1 Timothy 6:17
[380] See Matthew 5:44-45
[381] Proverbs 3:9-10, (emphasis added)

or tenth. Under the Rule of Grace, God simply gives gifts, there is no merit on the part of the receiver, so that "nobody can boast."

Ironically, most congregations quote John 3:16 – "For God so loved the world that he gave his one and only Son, that whoever *believes* in him shall not perish but have eternal life,"[382] – and still miss the open message of Grace in it. The Grace of God in this verse is in two respects: As a matter of gift – "gave his one and only Son" – and the absence of legalism or sacrifice, only belief – "whoever believes in him shall not perish but have eternal life."

John 3:16 has never been a conditional invitation; it is a completed work. God has already "given" His Son (He is not promising to give His Son if we do certain things; Jesus was given for all of humanity and publicly crucified, died and rose again). The condition is not in the giving, the condition is in the receiving.

This is a fundamental change from the Old Covenant where the condition was prior to the giving. Under the Rule of Grace, God gave before He was even asked, and He pleads with people to receive the gift already given. Law ensured that no gift was given unless certain conditions were met, Grace has given before there is any evidence of request. The gift is available

---

[382] John 3:16 (emphasis added)

to all who will believe and receive it. There is, therefore, no external requirement to satisfy the will of the giver – there is only a willingness to receive what has already been given. That is, Grace does not demand perfection before there is a bequeathing of blessing or benefit. Grace bequeaths blessings and gifts first, regardless of the condition of the recipient. Both the sinner and the saint are entitled to the benefits under Grace.

It is amazing that people fear to offend the church's sources of income. Tactics like "God will bless you if you tithe. God will pour into your bosom when you tithe. Tithing is an act of worship. Tithing builds your faith. Tithing breaks the power of greed," and similarly-situated gestures, are not based on real New Testament teaching. It is better to write the truth of modern tithing culture that it is a form of financial support for the work. Indeed, "tithing" provides for ministry financial support, and is not based on any spiritual obligations.

As argued above, it may suitably be described as giving for the operations of the congregation, such as paying pastor's salary, rentals, and etc. It is never given in the New Testaments, if practiced in a church, as a form of spiritual homage. That ended with the Old Covenant. God does not punish anyone for failure to give tithe under the Rule of Grace.

No-one is cursed who does not give

tithe. In the Old Testament, it was a duty to obey the entire Law otherwise one was under a curse for failure to do so: "'Cursed be anyone who does not confirm the words of this law by doing them.' And all the people shall say, 'Amen.'"[383] If anyone insists on adherence to tithing as an ablution of divine efficacy, it portends hypocritical for all intentions and purposes. Galatians 3:10 is even more explicit: "For all who rely on the works of the law are under a curse, as it is written: 'Cursed is everyone who does not continue to do *everything* written in the Book of the Law'" (emphasis added).

The oft-made argument is that tithing is pre-law and, therefore, it is not part of the Law. This argument still falls short under the Rule of Grace. This assertion supports the very premise it purports to undermine. If tithing was pre-law, it, therefore, follows that, then as now, tithing could be seen as a work of Grace. Abram gave a tenth to Melchizedek out of his own volition (willingness); it was never commanded to him to do so. Under the Mosaic Law, however, it became a command. Either way, tithing seems to be obsolete, both based on pre-law or the law or post-law observances.

Proponents of the tithing doctrine advise that tithing should be given to the

---

[383] Deuteronomy 27:26

"storehouse" or the church. They warn of giving it to media evangelists or freelance ministries or charitable organizations. They are right; it should not be given to those entities, neither is it to be given to a church. Paul illustrates that a New Testament Minister ought to work with his or her own hands. In his testimony to the elders, Paul writes:

> I have not coveted anyone's silver or gold or clothing. You yourselves know that these hands of mine have supplied my own needs and the needs of my companions. In everything I did, I showed you that by this kind of hard work we must help the weak, remembering the words the Lord Jesus himself said: 'It is more blessed to give than to receive.[384]

Moreover, Paul discloses, "We work hard with our own hands."[385] Paul advises the Corinthians, "You should mind your own business and work with your hands, just as we told you, so that your daily life may win the respect of outsiders and so that you will not be dependent on anybody."[386] And in his strongest words ever, Paul commands:

---

[384] Acts 20: 33-35
[385] 1 Corinthians 4:12
[386] 1 Thessalonians 4:11-12

> In the name of the Lord Jesus Christ, we command you, brothers and sisters, to keep away from every believer who is idle and disruptive and does not live according to the teaching you received from us. For you yourselves know how you ought to follow our example. We were not idle when we were with you, nor did we eat anyone's food without paying for it. On the contrary, we worked night and day, laboring and toiling so that we would not be a burden to any of you. We did this, not because we do not have the right to such help, but in order to offer ourselves as a model for you to imitate. For even when we were with you, we gave you this rule: 'The one who is unwilling to work shall not eat. We hear that some among you are idle and disruptive. They are not busy; they are busybodies. Such people we command and urge in the Lord Jesus Christ to settle down and earn the food they eat.[387]

It is wiser to ask the church to give a special offering or offerings to cover the expenses of operating a Ministry or church business. It is wiser to be candid and tell the truth. The allure tithing provides is that it is a

---

[387] 2 Thessalonians 3: 6-11

dependable and sustainable form of revenue to the church. Ten percent of all income the congregants get can go a long way to meeting the payroll and other needs of the church. However, tithing should not be used as a weapon to force people to give. People, under the Rule of Grace, can give even more than ten percent of their income, if they are willing to do so without compulsion. But they can also give less than ten percent. Still, they can choose not to give at all. In all of these circumstances, they have not committed sin, violated a principle or disobeyed a command. It is just as simple as that: Tithing is not sanctioned under the Rule of Grace.

It is not in conformity with the teachings of the New Testament to consider people who do not give tithes as greedy, ignorant, rebellious, or unbelievers. These may not fail to give tithe due to personal debt, either. It is simply not permitted under the Rule of Grace.

Some of those who advocate for tithing, do reinvest what they collect from tithes into other businesses or properties they may own. This would be fundamentally against the Levitical mandate. In pre-law, Abram was already rich in cattle, in silver, and in gold[388] when he gave a tithe to Melchizedek. In fact, Abram gave Melchizedek a tenth of everything and Abram is blessed in *Genesis*

---

[388] See Genesis 13:2

14, after we are told that Abram is already rich in *Genesis 13*.

And during the Law Period, those who received tithe would not diversify it into other businesses or own property or lands.

Pairing tithing with divine law, in New Testament times, does not meet the Grace criteria, no matter how subtle tithing advocates would like to be.

This is the hallmark of the Pauline Theology on giving:

> Consider this: Whoever sows sparingly will also reap sparingly, and whoever sows generously will also reap generously. *Each one should give what he has decided in his heart to give, not out of regret or compulsion. For God loves a cheerful giver.* And God is able to make all grace abound to you, so that in all things, at all times, having all that you need, you will abound in every good work."[389]

Notice that no percentage is given, and God is not the decider of how much someone must give, if giving at all. The crucial principle exemplified here is that the giver determines how much they must give. The one who gives (sows) more, reaps more. There is nothing new with this principle; it exists freely in nature. Farmers

---

[389] 2 Corinthians 9: 6-8, (emphasis added)

are very conversant with this principle. No-one should be compelled or forced to give. God loves those who decide to give, and give they do, cheerfully.

There is a danger to corrupting the context and teaching people that tithing is a regular or was a regular collection habit of the Early Church. This is usually linked to 1 Corinthians 16:2, "Now about the collection for the saints, you are to do as I directed the churches of Galatia: *On the first day of every week, each of you should set aside a portion of his income*, saving it up, so that when I come no collections will be needed. Then, on my arrival, I will send letters with those you recommend to carry your *gift* to Jerusalem" (emphasis added). This is not an authority to collect *tithes* in the New Testament.

First, it was not a regular occurrence. Apostle Paul never collected from the Corinthians each week; he did it for a particular project. His instructions were to collect a *particular portion* each week until enough was collected for the Jerusalem Church. It was not a tithe that they collected; it was a regular offering and it depended on each giver's willingness to give their own pre-determined portion. And that project had a beginning and would, definitely, come to an end. It was not to be a continuous practice of the Early Church under the Rule of Grace.

Second, Paul does not instruct people to

set aside a tenth of their incomes, even in this specific context. He leaves it open-ended for people to determine how much they are willing to give. This is in harmony with the teaching of Grace under the Pauline Theology.

And third, Paul calls the collection a "gift." This is antagonistic to Law – where adherents were expected to carry out the activity as a matter of obedience to the law. A gift, on the other hand, is determined by the giver and does not confer continuity.

Under Grace, the one who tithes or gives and the one who does not, both have equal standing in Christ before God: "But I tell you, love your enemies and pray for those who persecute you, that you may be sons of your Father in Heaven. *He causes His sun to rise on the evil and the good, and sends rain on the righteous and the unrighteous.*"[390]

Arguments may be made that these kinds of verses speak to the spiritual blessings and not monetary blessings. It is true that all are blessed spiritually who put their trust in God through Christ: "Praise be to the God and Father of our Lord Jesus Christ, who *has blessed us in the heavenly realms with every spiritual blessing* in Christ."[391] However, Grace gives more than money; it elevates us to excellence in everything: "But since you excel in *everything* – in faith, in

---

[390] Matthew 5:44-45, (emphasis added)
[391] Ephesians 1:3, (emphasis added)

speech, in knowledge, in complete earnestness and in the love we have kindled in you -- see that you also excel in this grace of giving."[392] Spiritual blessings are superior to any form or type of blessings.[393] A blessing by definition is anything that is not a curse; it is not money or wealth. Money and wealth may be blessings or curses depending on the attitude or spiritual or moral disposition of the possessor and the use and purpose for which money and wealth are put to. Some people may have plenty of money and wealth and choose to hate or harm others or despise or abuse others with it. Money and wealth are amoral; they are neither good nor bad. The one who has a lot of it is, therefore, the determinative factor.

Spiritual blessings are embedded in these passages: "And do not be conformed to this world, but be transformed by the renewing of your mind, so that you may prove what the will of God is, that which is good and acceptable and perfect. Therefore, I urge you, brethren, by the mercies of God, to present your bodies a living and holy sacrifice, acceptable to God, which is your spiritual service of worship."[394] We become more like Christ Jesus when we are sanctified to God – when we are set apart for His purposes. As the Bible also says,

---

[392] 2 Corinthians 8:7
[393] See footnote 367, *infra*.
[394] Romans 12:1-2

"And we know that God causes all things to work together for good to those who love God, to those who are called according to His purpose."[395] To love God and to be called according to His purpose are spiritual blessings.

Other types of spiritual blessings are illustrated below, thus:

> But someone will say, "How are the dead raised? And with what kind of body do they come?" You fool! That which you sow does not come to life unless it dies; and that which you sow, you do not sow the body which is to be, but a bare grain, perhaps of wheat or of something else. But God gives it a body just as He wished, and to each of the seeds a body of its own. All flesh is not the same flesh, but there is one flesh of men, and another flesh of beasts, and another flesh of birds, and another of fish. There are also heavenly bodies and earthly bodies, but the glory of the heavenly is one, and the glory of the earthly is another. There is one glory of the sun, and another glory of the moon, and another glory of the stars; for star differs from star in glory. So also, it is written, "The first MAN, Adam, BECAME A

---

[395] Romans 8:28

LIVING SOUL " The last Adam became a life giving spirit. However, the spiritual is not first, but the natural; then the spiritual. *The first man is from the earth, earthy; the second man is from Heaven. As is the earthy, so also are those who are earthy; and as is the heavenly, so also are those who are heavenly.* Just as we have borne the image of the earthy, we will also bear the image of the heavenly. Now I say this, brethren, that flesh and blood cannot inherit the kingdom of God; nor does the perishable inherit the imperishable. Behold, I tell you a mystery; we will not all sleep, but we will all be changed, in a moment, in the twinkling of an eye, at the last trumpet; for the trumpet will sound, and the dead will be raised imperishable, and we will be changed. For this perishable must put on the imperishable, and this mortal must put on immortality.

But when this perishable will have put on the imperishable, and this mortal will have put on immortality, then will come about the saying that is written, "Death is consumed in victory. "Death, where is your victory? O death, where is your sting?" The sting of death is sin, and the power of sin is the law; but thanks be to God, who gives us the victory through

> our Lord Jesus Christ. Therefore, my beloved brethren, be steadfast, immovable, always abounding in the work of the Lord, knowing that your toil is not in vain in the Lord.[396]

It is important to see how Paul renders the nexus between our spiritual destiny to Law and Grace. He alludes to our real destiny – to be reunited with Christ in glory. However, he is also concerned with the barrier that stands in between – namely, that sin, strengthened by Law, is a menace that puts our spiritual destiny at risk. God has a solution for that. It is called Grace. Paul praises God that through Christ, through His grace, we have overcome the world. In this passage, we also notice that the "power of sin is the law." To deal with the power of sin, something better and stronger than the Law was required. God found it in Grace. Grace is above the Law, literally.

What Grace does is to pre-empt the Law, so that the Law has no power of sin over human souls. God is able to redeem humankind without any obedience to any law except the Law of Grace. The Dispensation of Grace is the Rule of Grace, as opposed to the Rule of Law. If there is no law, the power of sin is nulled. If there is law, there is sin. Grace is the antidote

---

[396] 1 Corinthians 15:35-58

against sin, because it does not afford sin an avenue to get stronger. Under Grace, there is nothing to violate; there is no law to break.

Grace is all-encompassing: "For in Him you have been *enriched in every way*, in all speech and all knowledge."[397] Grace makes us rich without tithing or giving – that is why it is more superior to law. Under the Law of Moses, the Israelites were required to tithe every year – to hold elaborate feasts and festivals – under Grace, God freely supplies the grace.

Christ Jesus our Lord brought us Grace to enrich us in every way – to be rich "in every way": "For you know the grace of our Lord Jesus Christ, that though he was rich, yet for your sake he became poor, so that you through his poverty might become rich."[398] There is no mincing of words, here richness is simply richness and it means richness in resources and money. It is the very opposite of poverty. Jesus has brought us Grace to be rich. We need not do anything to satisfy the law, except to believe in Jesus Christ and transact in righteousness.[399] If we insist that to access God's richness we need to tithe, then it is no longer of Grace; it becomes of works. For Christ to become poor and we simply take on His richness – that, then, is the true

---

[397] 1 Corinthians 1:5
[398] 2 Corinthians 8:9
[399] See Matthew 6:33

meaning of Grace. And God has not ended at Christ's imputing of His Grace unto us, God continues – He is able – to make that Grace abound towards us in everything, always: "And God is able to make all grace abound to you, so that in all things, at all times, having all that you need, you will abound in every good work."[400]

It is important to note here that the Bible is clear: "…so that in all things, at all times, having all that you need, you will abound in every good work," means that if you own property, it is protected. If you have crops, they are covered. If you have animals, they bear more. If you have a job, it is safe. If you have a business, it is well. All this must be at God's whim and not ours, otherwise it is not of Grace. All we need to do is believe that all shall be and is well and rave in His Grace for us.

Grace does not justify waste, laziness or lethargy. Grace is reasonable and diligent, and we ought to be occupied as He is occupied: "He who is faithful in what is least is faithful also in much; and he who is unjust in what is least is unjust also in much. Therefore, if you have not been faithful in the unrighteous mammon, who will commit to your trust the true riches?"[401] Grace will give us all things but we must be faithful managers of what God has given us.

---

[400] 2 Corinthians 9:8
[401] Luke 16:10-11

Grace does not make us irresponsible; it gives the power to be industrious, enterprising and versatile.

Grace, Tithing and the New Testament

The general rule is that if there is a new, the old, ought, of necessity, to be obsolete. However, in morality and theology, the old may still give efficacy to the new in terms of principles. While we may infer the total absolution of the Old Testament in practice, in principle, however, we still need the saliences and moral structure they enforced. As argued in this treatise, the principle underlying tithing was obedience and not enrichment.

God is materially rich: "'The silver is mine and the gold is mine,' declares the LORD Almighty."[402] In essence and in practicality, all things come from God: "But who am I and who are my people that we should be able to offer as generously as this? For all things come from You, and from Your hand we have given You…O LORD our God, all this abundance that we have provided to build You a house for Your holy name, it is from Your hand, and all is Yours."[403]

In fact, even the earth itself is the Lord's: "The earth is the LORD's, and

---

[402] Haggai 2:8
[403] 1 Chronicles 29:14, 16

everything in it, the world, and all who live in it."[404] The flora and fauna are the Lord's, too: "For all the animals of the forest are mine, and I own the cattle on a thousand hills."[405] Common-sense surely dictates that God is materially rich. He created everything, and what He created is good: "For everything God created is good, and nothing is to be rejected if it is received with thanksgiving…"[406] For, "The earth is the Lord's, and the fullness thereof."[407] God not only created everything – "The God who made the world and everything in it is the Lord of heaven and earth and does not live in temples made by human hands,"[408] – but He also gives life to everything: "This is what God the LORD says – the Creator of the heavens, who stretches them out, who spreads out the earth with all that springs from it, who gives breath to its people, and life to those who walk on it."[409]

The New Testament is the truest Dispensation of Grace: "If ye have heard of the dispensation of the grace of God which is given me to you-ward."[410] There is also no question that we are no longer under Law: "But now we are released from the

---

[404] Psalm 24:1
[405] Psalm 50:10
[406] 1 Timothy 4:4
[407] 1 Corinthians 10:26
[408] Acts 17:24
[409] Isaiah 42:5
[410] Ephesians 3:2, KJB

law, having died to that which held us captive, so that we serve in the new way of the Spirit and not in the old way of the written code [law]."[411] Law captured and imprisoned them and the Spirit has released and freed us. Now we rest on Grace, not Law: "Therefore, the promise comes by faith, so that it may rest on grace and may be guaranteed to all Abraham's offspring – not only to those who are of the law, but also to those who are of the faith of Abraham. He is the father of us all."[412] We are of Abraham's type, not of Moses type. The Mosaic laws are still persuasive, but they are not binding upon those who are of the faith of Abraham.

Many Old Testament principles have been transposed onto the New Testament. However, many Old Testament practices have been discontinued. The practice of tithing has neither been continued nor sustained in the New Testament. The New Testament does not advocate for the continuation of the tithing regime, in word or in spirit. However, its principle of obedience is still germane today.

The Bible verses oft-referred to in the New Testament as justifying tithing are both narrow in scope and too widely interpreted. In short, they fall short of the truth test inherent in holistic biblical

---

[411] Romans 7:6, (English Standard Version)
[412] Romans 4:16, (Berean Study Bible)

interpretation. In Matthew, Jesus rebukes, "Woe to you, scribes and Pharisees, hypocrites! For you pay tithe of mint and anise and cummin, and have neglected the weightier matters of the law: Justice and mercy and faith. These you ought to have done, without leaving the others undone."[413]

First, and according to our Lord, there was weightier and lighter matters of the Law. Justice, mercy and faith were ranked higher than giving tithes.

Second, Jesus was speaking during the Dispensation of Law – and even during that time, tithing was not a weightier matter. In Luke, the same argument is captured: "But woe to you Pharisees! For you tithe mint and rue and all manner of herbs, and pass by justice and the love of God. These you ought to have done, without leaving the others undone."[414] To justice, mercy, and faith, our Lord added the love of God. And these are weightier ("ought to be done") matters of the Law.

But remember that our Lord was still making commentary on matters of the Old Testament, for at that time, the New Testament was not in effect (Christ had not died and resurrected yet). Our Lord spoke those words in harmony with the directives of the Old Agreement (Testament). And we

---

[413] Matthew 23:23
[414] Luke 11:42

do not hear from Christ on this issue until His apostles and disciples begin to preach the message of the New Testament. It is under this Dispensation of Grace by His apostles that we become fully aware of the meaning of all that Jesus said and did.

The position of Christ in relation to the existing Old Testament is illustrated in the following: "But when the fullness of the time had come, God sent forth His Son, born of a woman, born under the law, to redeem those who were under the law."[415] All the words He uttered and miracles He performed, He did under the umbrella of the Old Testament. For example, in Matthew 8, we observe, "And immediately his leprosy was cleansed. See that you tell no one; but go your way, show yourself to the priest, and offer the gift that Moses commanded, as a testimony to them."[416] Our Lord ordered compliance with the Mosaic Law at that time because He was operating under the Law:

> For the same reason He compelled tithing in Matthew 23:23. The Law of Moses was still in force during the life of Christ. It would have been 'sin' for Christ at this time to have taught against the Law of Moses! In the Matthew 23:23 and Luke 11:42 verses

---

[415] Galatians 4:4-5
[416] Matthew 8:3-4

> Christ was not teaching that tithing was required by the New Testament, but rather was just re-enforcing that this was a requirement under the Old Covenant.[417]

It is very difficult to justify tithing in the New Testament. The temptation has always been for Ministers and church leaders to attempt to link tithing through the eyes of Grace. Thus, many verses of Scripture in the Old Testament on tithing are explained in the light of twisted "giving verses" in the New Testament. This error, though not eternally damning, is injurious to the principle and purposes of Grace.

When a Pharisee prays, "I fast twice in the week, I give tithes of all that I possess,"[418] it is not an attestation to the continuation of tithing under the New Testament. Indeed, the Pharisees operated under the Law during Jesus' ministry on earth. It is, rather, an illustration of what self-righteousness and pride can produce. Our Lord was emphasizing mercy – a weightier matter in the Law than tithing.

And often times, New Testament verses are twisted to give effect to the efficacy of tithing. A good example is Hebrews 7:

---

[417] Tithing in the New Testament (http://www.bibleinsight.com/ti-new-testament-tithing.html - retrieved: February 22nd, 2018)
[418] Luke 18:12

> Consider how great Melchizedek was: Even the patriarch Abraham gave him a tenth of the spoils. Now the Law commands the sons of Levi who become priests to collect a tenth from the people (that is, their brothers), even though they are descended from Abraham. But Melchizedek, who did not trace his descent from Levi, collected a tenth from Abraham and blessed him who had the promises. And indisputably, the lesser is blessed by the greater. In the case of the Levites, mortal men collect the tenth; but in the case of Melchizedek, it is affirmed that he lives on. And so, to speak, Levi, who collects the tenth, paid the tenth through Abraham. For when Melchizedek met Abraham, Levi was still in the loin of his ancestor.[419]

Abraham paid tithes to Melchizedek directly. Melchizedek was a type of Christ. The Levites under the Old Testament received tithes from the people. The lesser was blessed by the greater. However, the critical review of this passage of scripture centers on the identity of Melchizedek and the changing priesthood under the New

---

[419] Hebrews 7:4-10

Testament. As a consequence, tithing under the Old Testament is discussed, but not tithing under the New Testament.

There is no clarification given to tithing in the New Testament in this passage, either. If for argument sake, and by analogy, the transfer of authority be extended to the New Testament, there will still be a problem. That problem is that if we are to pay tithing under the order of Melchizedek, we would, therefore, be required to tithe directly to Christ. We would not be tithing through church appointed Ministers or church leaders. This would eliminate any representations on behalf of Christ.

For the New Testament, we do not access God by representation of any human agent; we do so directly to God. The five-fold ministers are not intermediaries; they are fellow members of the Body of Christ with us. God now resides in us through the Holy Spirit.

Moreover, as already argued under "Tithe in Pre-Law Period," Abram did tithe out of his abundance. It was an illustration of what tithe, or any other form of giving, might look like under Grace. Abram tithed after victory, not before it. In short, Abram did not tithe as a way of attracting blessings, Abram was already blessed by Melchizedek when he gave his tithe.[420]

The Apostles, especially under the

---

[420] See Genesis 14:18-20

Paulin Theology, go to lengths to belabor this issue. There was no specific command to the new believers to tithe:

> And now I commit you to God and to the *word of His grace*, which can build you up and give you an inheritance among all who are sanctified. I have not coveted anyone's silver or gold or clothing. You yourselves know that these hands of mine have ministered to my own needs and those of my companions. In everything, I showed you that by this kind of hard work we must help the weak, remembering the words of the Lord Jesus Himself: 'It is more blessed to give than to receive.[421]

Perhaps of all God's workers Paul could have qualified as a true royal priest,[422] and, therefore be a subject of receipt of tithes. If the modern church leaders collect tithes, Paul could collect more. However, Paul defends his record of receiving alms and gifts, including tithes. Paul did the following: He did not covet silver, gold or clothing; he worked hard on his own; and

---

[421] Acts 20:32-35 (emphasis added)
[422] See 1 Peter 2:9" "But you are a chosen people, a royal priesthood, a holy nation, God's special possession, that you may declare the praises of him who called you out of darkness into his wonderful light" (NIV).

he gave more than he received. Surely, if the tithing regime was that effectual, Paul would not have to labor very hard on his own; he would have concentrated on prayer, preaching and teaching. But, as noted here, Paul worked as hard as he prayed, preached and taught the Word of God. He did this, as again he notes, because he was committed to the "the word of His grace," and not to the dictates and the letter of Law of Moses.

Paul continues the same argument: "I robbed other churches, taking wages from them to minister to you. And when I was present with you, and in need, I was a burden to no-one, for what was lacking to me the brethren who came from Macedonia supplied."[423]

And again:

> The only thing I failed to do, which I do in the other churches, *was to become a financial burden to you. Please forgive me for this wrong!* See, I am ready to come to you a third time, and I will not be a burden, because I am not seeking your possessions, but you yourselves. For children should not have to save up for their parents, but parents for their children. And for the sake of your souls, I will most gladly spend my money and

---

[423] 2 Corinthians 11:8-9

> myself. If I love you more, will you love me less?"[424]

Paul apologized to this church that he had become a burden to them because he asked them for money. The fact that he issued an apology is detailing of the fact that, under Grace, he should not have to burden the church by seeking financial gifts. The veracity of this verse of Scripture is that Paul's humility is at deep display. He did not ask for money for himself, he was asking for the help of other churches.

Then Paul unleashes the real crux of the Grace message vis-à-vis finances and giving:

> For it is superfluous for me to write to you about this ministry to the saints; for I know your readiness, of which I boast about you to the Macedonians, namely, that Achaia has been prepared since last year, and your zeal has stirred up most of them. But I have sent the brethren, in order that our boasting about you may not be made empty in this case, so that, as I was saying, you may be prepared; otherwise if any Macedonians come with me and find you unprepared, we -- not to speak of you -- will be put to shame by this confidence. So, I thought it necessary to urge the

---

[424] 2 Corinthians 12:13-15

> brethren that they would go on ahead to you and arrange beforehand your previously promised bountiful gift, so that the same would be ready as a bountiful gift and not affected by covetousness. Now this I say, *he who sows sparingly will also reap sparingly, and he who sows bountifully will also reap bountifully. Each one must do just as he has purposed in his heart, not grudgingly or under compulsion, for God loves a cheerful giver.* And God is able to make all grace abound to you, so that always having all sufficiency in everything, you may have an abundance for every good deed....[425]

Tithe is not mentioned nor alluded to in this discourse. But it is the principle underlying New Testament giving (all manner of giving) that is at play here. As Paul spells out, it must be willful giving, without grudging, and not under compulsion; because "God loves a cheerful giver."[426] Tithing was not a willful giving; it was a legal requirement under the Mosaic Law. If tithing has to conform to the New Testament Grace Dispensation, it must be willful, and given without compulsion or

---

[425] 2 Corinthians 9:1-8, New American Standard Version (emphasis added)
[426] 2 Corinthians 9:7

force. It should emanate from people's hearts, and not from a legalistic requirement to give a tenth of one's income.

Paul advocated for principle of equality in giving. The have-nots should not outgive the haves, and vice versa:

> For if there is first a willing mind, it is accepted according to what one has, and not according to what he does not have. For I do not mean that others should be eased and you burdened; but by an equality, that now at this time your abundance may supply their lack, that their abundance also may supply your lack – that there may be equality.[427]

Paul is not the first to observe equality of giving, our Lord also did: "Jesus called His disciples to Him and said, 'Truly I tell you, this poor widow has put more than all the others into the treasury. For they all contributed out of their surplus, but she out of her poverty has put in all she had to live on.'"[428]

It should be noted that Jesus was not recommending giving beyond one's means, or more than one owned or had. He was barely stating a fact of the hypocrisy of the rich he had observed. They had given what

---

[427] 2 Corinthians 8:12-14
[428] Mark 12:43-44

looked to be a lot, but if considered together and in context, the poor widow gave more. Paul made a clarification, namely, that there should be equality in giving. The fundamental principle of giving, as reiterated by Paul again above, is that any form of alms-giving, offering, and even a tithe, if it existed in the New Testament, ought to be out of a willing heart and "according to what one has, and not according to what he does not have." That is the message of Grace.

Paul was very clear on the requirement by the congregation to contribute to the material needs of Gospel Ministers and church leaders. In other words, the Church needs money to function and Paul recognized that. All the preaching that money is required to "advance the Kingdom of God" are correct. However, it is the method of fundraising that is questionable in the New Testament. Accordingly, any form of giving that is willful and not with compulsion is welcome in the Church. In fact, it is imperative that Christian ministry is operated like a business if it has to manipulate scarce resources and win many souls.[429] Those who work for God deserve, and have the right, to be compensated in material things:

---

[429] Read, Charles Mwewa, *Christian Ministry as Business: Ten Principle Guidelines to Maximize Ministry Profitability* (Ottawa: ACP, 2021) for a comprehensive study on ministry and finances.

> If we have sown spiritual seed among you, is it too much if we reap a material harvest from you? If others have this right of support from you, shouldn't we have it all the more? But we did not use this right. On the contrary, we put up with anything rather than hinder the gospel of Christ. Don't you know that those who serve in the temple get their food from the temple, and that those who serve at the altar share in what is offered on the altar? In the same way, the Lord has commanded that those who preach the gospel should receive their living from the gospel.[430]

This is a noble message. Paul does encourage industry and creativity in the Church. But he speculates that this might be abused by the busy-bodied Ministers. Those who preach should live by the Gospel, just like those who do secular jobs do depend on those jobs for material survival. If tithe is used as a method of collecting money for the preaching of the Gospel, this should be stated so. And it should be made very clear that this is a policy of that particular congregation and not a requirement under the biblical order.

If people decide to give a tenth of all

---

[430] 1 Corinthians 9:11-14

their income, it should meet the same New Testament standard; it should be volitional, willful, without compulsion, and according to one's means and ability. It is not sin; it is not disobedience in the New Testament not to tithe. But it is a good thing to do, to share in good things with those who live to teach and preach the Word of God: "Let him who is taught the word share in all good things with him who teaches."[431] "All good things" here is not only limited to money – it may include all other material things.

It is acceptable in the New Testament, under Grace, for a Minister of the Gospel to receive wages from the ministry, and if they are traveling evangelists, from other congregations. It is equally very commendable that they work and supply their own needs. It is cautioned under the New Testament to place any monetary burden solely upon the congregation. In the same vein, if giving is institutionalized in any particular congregation, it must be proportionate to people's ability to give. In other words, there must be equality of giving; no-one or one party should be unnecessarily burdened.

Furthermore, if one part of the globe is hit by natural disasters or famine or any form of misfortune, the believers in well-to-do places and countries or churches should

---

[431] Galatians 6:6

help those in need. It is a New Testament phenomenon to engage in philanthropy as well as in goodwill giving, and even in televised charitable programs. The only caveat, as Paul teaches, is such giving should not be abused or misused for personal gain or aggrandizement.

A prophet of God can even foretell that there would be disasters to prepare God's people for action: "In those days some prophets came down from Jerusalem to Antioch. One of them named Agabus stood up and predicted through the Spirit that a great famine would sweep across the entire Roman world" (This happened under Claudius).[432]

Similarly, churches and Christian programs can target the poor and provide help: "For Macedonia and Achaia were pleased to make a contribution for the poor among the Lord's people in Jerusalem."[433] And Paul was very clear that Christians could receive financial support and contributions from non-believers if those non-believers have benefited from their Gospel: "For if the Gentiles have shared in their spiritual blessings, they are obligated to minister to them with material blessings."[434] The principle is: Those involved in preaching the Gospel should be financially rewarded by those receiving the

---

[432] Acts 11:27-28
[433] Romans 15:26
[434] Romans 15:27

message.

The central argument, though, still remains, that tithe is not a commanded New Testament method for financial sourcing. The tithing principle does not have a spiritually or morally binding force under Grace. It can be a persuasive policy for ministerial budgetary needs, but this should be clearly explained to the ministry or congregation.

Indeed, "For Scripture says, 'Do not muzzle an ox while it is treading out the grain,' and 'The worker deserves his wages.'"[435] Those who work full time in the church or ministry must be paid a salary. Their service should conform to available employment standards and guidelines in place in any particular nation or territory. And the assumption is that the church or ministry will have sufficient resources to meet the salary needs of its full time employees, Gospel ministers included.

However, if someone is starting or running a church or ministry, they may have to inform the congregation that their needs will be met through church offerings. If a *tithe* will be collected, the church or ministry must be informed similarly that the purpose of such a tithe is purely administrative and financial, and not to threaten them with the divine robbing mantras. The people deserve to know that under Grace, tithing is not an

---

[435] 1 Timothy 5:18

instituted church order.

Similarly, those who wish to enter into full time ministry, must understand that hard work will be required of them. If they can work and earn their own revenues, let them do so. If, however, they are unable to earn a living while working full time for the church or ministry, and if they want to give themselves fully to the preaching of the Word of God and to prayer, they should enter into an employment contract with their congregation and receive a salary for their labor. In the latter situation, the congregation may designate a *tithe* collection to compensate the Minister or church workers.

The New Testament leadership did not always request monetary assistance, if the Corinthian Model is to be critically examined. They did that if and when there was need. They did not collect tithe as we know it in the Early New Testament Church. The New Testament does not teach that, either. This is because the New Testament is a quintessential Grace dispensation.

In Summary

The best model New Testament churches should follow is treating tithing as a matter of canon (ecclesiastical) law and not divine or moral law. Canon or ecclesiastical law still applies to the management of church affairs under Grace. Churches and ministries can enact policies and guidelines on financial sourcing, including setting a tithe aside. But this should be based purely on unbinding canonical rules or by-laws and not the Mosaic or ceremonial law.

> O Lord, O love, our Great Father
> The riches of life You doeth gather
> For the children of Thine house,
> Thou hast served blessings to smouse.
> Grace, fully maketh us free from a tithe,
> To revert thereto will be but blithe;
> For all is permitted and is volitional,
> None's, serve to believe, conditional.

10 | PRAYER AND GRACE

The Old Meets the New

There is a distinction between prayer as it was practiced under the Old Testament and the way it is supposed to be under Grace. Under the Rule of Grace, prayer is a celebration of the already completed works of Christ. It is a response to what God has already done. Under the Dispensation of Grace, "…we know that in all things God works for the good of those who love him, who have been called according to his purpose."[436]

Grace has bequeathed to us an attitude of thanksgiving in relation to prayer. This is a wide change from a conditional approach to prayer akin to the old order. Under the Law, prayer was based on the fulfillment of some pre-conditions. The supplicant had to show that they had fulfilled certain steps or conditions before God could answer them. From time to time, God, through some holy people, invoked the Grace order in the Old Testament. However, this was prospective – it was looking forward to what God would do in future. That future is now. We are no longer under the Law but

---

[436] Romans 8:28

under Grace. Therefore, we should not approach God in the same way they did under the Law.

Under His illustrious example of how we should pray, Jesus starts at the point of grace – "Our Father." The Old Testament prayers were addressed to God based on rank or order. Our Lord Jesus changed all that. We now come to our Father. We do not relate to Him as a distant, unapproachable God; our relationship is now in-house. And God has already answered us in principle – for He did not spare His Son.[437]

Our only attitude to prayer is that of thanksgiving. Under Grace, every asking we do, we receive; every seeking we do, we find; and every knocking we undertake results in doors opening: "Ask and it will be given to you; seek and you will find; knock and the door will be opened to you."[438]

Thus, our New Testament order is to pray without stopping.[439] The praying-always, always gets results. Under Grace, we determine when we should have anything from God; we simply pray. Under Law, God determined when they should have anything, even after heavy fasting, floundering in sack clothing and ashes.[440]

---

[437] See Romans 8:32
[438] Matthew 7:7
[439] 1 Thessalonians 5:16-18
[440] See Genesis 37:34, 2 Samuel 3:31, Job 16:15, Lamentations 2:10, 1 Kings 21:27, 1 Chronicles

Under Grace, even fasting takes on a dignified, majestic and heroic gesture: "When you fast, do not look somber as the hypocrites do, for they disfigure their faces to show others they are fasting. Truly I tell you, they have received their reward in full. But when you fast, anoint your head and wash your face."[441]

Under Grace, our response to gift-giving is thanksgiving, happiness, gratitude, and the like. Grace is a system of gift-giving. Rather than, if you do this you will have that (conditional), under Grace, it becomes, you do have this (unconditionally). This means that the way we pray under the Dispensation of Grace is different from what they prayed under the Law. For example, II Chronicles 7:14 should now be rendered differently under Grace. Conditionally, if God's people repented, prayed and turned away from sins, God would answer and heal their land. Now, we simply pray and God answers.

This was predicted in Jeremiah 33:3, "Call to me and I will answer you and tell you great and unsearchable things you do not know." In Hebrew the word *chen* (grace) was used, and it focused on the future. The people of Israel looked to a future time when God would bequeath upon them unmerited favor. Under the New Testament

---

21:16, Nehemiah 9:1, Jonah 3:5-9, Isaiah 15:3, Jeremiah 49:3, Ezekiel 27:31, Matthew 11:21.
[441] Matthew 6:16-17

(Greek), the word is *charis* (gift) for Grace and it has a past reflection. We now reflect on the finished work of God; what God has already done through Christ our Lord. He sent His only Son to die for us and has granted us all gifts – "God has given each of you a gift from his great variety of spiritual gifts. Use them well to serve one another. Do you have the gift of speaking? Then speak as though God himself were speaking through you. Do you have the gift of helping others? Do it with all the strength and energy that God supplies. Then everything you do will bring glory to God through Jesus Christ. All glory and power to him forever and ever! Amen."[442] And Paul is explicit, "For it is by grace you have been saved, through faith—and this is not from yourselves, it is the gift of God."[443] It is not of works (verse 9), so no-one can boast, or take credit.

We have been justified (accepted) freely under the Dispensation of Grace. This means that we are all on the same playing field before God. No-one among us – as far as Grace is concerned – can claim that because of their gifts, abilities and a certain perchance, they have God's ear. God has loved us the same, regardless of what we have done. In fact, He loved us while we were not righteous, "But God demonstrates

---

[442] 1 Peter 4:10-11
[443] Ephesians 2:8

his own love for us in this: While we were still sinners, Christ died for us."[444] Christ died for us, not because we met a condition of righteousness or goodness, He died for us irrespective of our condition. He decided to die for us even when we were at enmity with Him. It was all unmerited favor, without condition and perfectly a matter of free gift.

The only condition we do have under Grace, it seems, is to pray in faith. Our Lord urged us to pray, "When you pray…."[445] And Paul beseeches us to pray without ceasing.[446] Both our Lord and His Apostle Paul alluded to the fact that we ought to always pray: "Then Jesus told his disciples a parable to show them that they should always pray and not give up,"[447] and "Therefore I want the men everywhere to pray, lifting up holy hands, without anger or dissension."[448]

This last verse also gives us the attitude of gracious praying, "without anger or dissension." New Testament praying is with faith and thanksgiving – because everything we have, will have or had are free gifts (Grace) from God. "All this is for your benefit, so that the grace that is reaching more and more people may cause

---

[444] Romans 5:8
[445] Mat. 6:9
[446] 1 Thessalonians 5:17
[447] Luke 18:1
[448] 1 Timothy 2:8

thanksgiving to overflow to the glory of God";[449] "Do not be anxious about anything, but in every situation, by prayer and petition, with thanksgiving, present your requests to God."[450] In terms of Grace and prayer, this verse of Scripture is the hallmark of all that the New Testament is all about. There is no need to be distressed or depressed or stressful. All we need is to pray, and prayer will trigger a peace that surpasses all understanding. And this is possible because we already have thanked God for the response by faith.

Moreover, "I always thank my God for you because of his grace given you in Christ Jesus";[451] "For this reason, ever since I heard about your faith in the Lord Jesus and your love for all God's people, I have not stopped giving thanks for you, remembering you in my prayers";[452] and "For everything God created is good, and nothing is to be rejected if it is received with thanksgiving, because it is consecrated by the word of God and prayer."[453]

God's Word (His word to us) and prayer (our words to Him) have the same effect under Grace. Food, for example, if poisoned, may be sanctified and rendered harmless by a prayer of faith. And this is

---

[449] 2 Corinthians 4:15
[450] Philippians 4:6
[451] 1 Corinthians 1:4
[452] Ephesians 1:15-16
[453] 1 Timothy 4:4-5

possible either by the Word of God or through prayer.

In Romans 8:32, we read: "He who did not spare his own Son, but gave him up for us all--how will he not also, along with him, graciously give us all things?" The phrase, "graciously give us all things" is detailing. Grace has given us all things in Christ. All means all. According to 2 Peter 1:3, "His divine power has given us everything we need for a godly life through our knowledge of him who called us by his own glory and goodness." See the rendition: "…given us everything… who called us by his own glory and goodness." All or everything means everything.

The combination of these two verses deduces the following three points:

First, that God was the first and last to make the initiative to give us things. We did not deserve the gifts. We did not qualify for them. We did not pay for them. We did not ask for them. We did not meet some conditions to get them. God, on His own accord, decided to give them to us. That is how Grace operates – God deciding to give us His benefits without us deserving any or all of them.

Second, God does give us all things because He first gave us His best. There is logic in this. If God or a human being, for that matter, is able to give his or her best, can they fail to give any other thing? Of course, not. Since God has already given us the best of life and nature, His only begotten Son.[454] He can give us all things together with Jesus our Lord. This, essentially, means that we have God's permission to receive anything we desire or ask of Him. This also means that God cannot deny us anything that is good for us. He has already given the best; He can give all other good gifts: "Every good and perfect gift is from above, coming down from the Father of the heavenly lights, who does not change like shifting shadows."[455] God gave the best; He will always give the good gifts under Grace.

Third, there is no human agent involved or a human deserving involved in God's gracious gifts. He gave us – we did not ask from Him. This is very notable. Under the Law, people petitioned, supplicated, beseeched, searched and fasted to have God move on their behalf.

They had to meet a set of standards – legal, moral and ceremonial – in order to appease God and invoke His blessings. Note further, "All these blessings will come on you and accompany you *if* you obey the LORD your God."[456]

Most people fail to reconcile the fact that God can bequeath all the blessings without us meeting a single condition. The above-quoted verse has been commented

---

[454] John 3:16
[455] James 1:17
[456] Deuteronomy 28:2 (emphasis added)

upon by the best Bible commentators worldwide and in many cases, more often than not these great thinkers quiver on the freedom to receive without any conditions. The Old Testament is obsolete as far as the method of blessings are concerned. Under the New Testament, the Dispensation of Grace, blessings have already been provided: "Praise be to the God and Father of our Lord Jesus Christ, who has blessed us in the heavenly realms with every spiritual blessing in Christ."[457] These blessings already given to us, freely, are more potent that the trivial and passing earthly blessings. Money, property and etc., are fleeting in comparison to spiritual blessings. These spiritual blessings are guaranteed for us in the presence of God. They are ours; they cannot be stolen from us. They are spiritual and are contained for us in the heavenly places. We do not need to ask for them; all we need is to appropriate them with thanks. A gift is not useful if it's not received. All we need to do is receive the gifts God has given us freely through Christ.

In Summary

---

[457] Ephesians 1:3

This chapter will be concluded with a discussion on the phrase, "in Christ." This speaks of the finished work of Christ. It's very important to pose and reflect on what it means by to "finish." It means finality. Christ will not do it again. He will not give us again. He has already given us.

In Christ, we have all blessings (spiritual and otherwise). Our provisions are past, present and future: "And God will generously provide all you need. Then you will always have everything you need and plenty left over to share with others."[458] This alludes to material blessings. That God will "generously" provide all things. God does so when we ask. The finality is contained in, "For you know the grace of our Lord Jesus Christ, that though he was rich, yet for your sake he became poor, so that you through his poverty might become rich."[459] Christ already became poor – was born (although He was God; he was born in a poor family; spent His years on earth living like a commoner and so on). This is what Christ decided to do to lower Himself to the level of humanity: "Who, existing in the form of God, did not consider equality with God something to be grasped, but emptied Himself, taking the form of a servant, being made in human likeness. And being found in appearance as a man, He

---

[458] 2 Corinthians 9:8
[459] 2 Corinthians 8:9

humbled Himself and became obedient to death—even death on a cross."[460] Christ did all these lowly things already. He became poor, and the good news is that, "so that you through his poverty might become rich."

A rich person is not the person who has money or wealth, it is a person who has access to all blessings. Christians in Christ have access to all material and divine blessings made available through Christ. This does not diminish even when a Christian is presently poor in material things. That is the secret of God. The blunt truth, however, is that Christians have both spiritual and material blessings in Christ.[461]

Moses gave the Law; Christ Jesus gave us Grace and truth, freely: "For the law was given through Moses; Grace and truth came through Jesus Christ."[462] We are not under the Law any longer. We received a free gift of Grace and truth when we accepted Christ Jesus. We have Grace to help us in our times of need. All we need to do is pray: "Let us then approach God's throne of grace with confidence [thanksgiving], so that we may receive mercy and find grace to

---

[460] Philippians 2:6-8
[461] The Theology of Material Blessings or why some people may not all the material blessings they need is widely covered throughout the New Testament and it has nothing to do with luck or hard work on our part.
[462] John 1:17

help us in our time of need."[463]

When we lack anything under Grace, we must pray. When we need provisions, we must pray. When we want something immediately, we ought to pray. That's the response to Grace as far as prayer is concerned: "Fear not, little flock, for it is your Father's good pleasure to give you the kingdom."[464] And He has given us already by Grace through faith in Jesus Christ.

Grace has guaranteed us acquittal in Christ: "Therefore there is now no condemnation at all for those who are in Christ Jesus."[465] This is total and final, no-one can bring an accusation against us. Apostle Paul poses a rhetorical question:

> Who is there to condemn us? For Christ Jesus, who died, and more than that was raised to life, is at the right hand of God—and He is interceding for us. Who shall separate us from the love of Christ? Shall trouble or distress or persecution or famine or nakedness or danger or sword? As it is written: "For Your sake we face death all day long; we are considered as sheep to be slaughtered." No, in all these things we are more than conquerors through Him who

---

[463] Hebrews 4:16
[464] Luke 12:32
[465] Romans 8:1

loved us.

And there can be no more illustration of quintessential Grace than in this passage. Grace has done the impossible; it has made the vulnerable lambs survive where tough lions perish. And it has stuck God's love to those who believe in Jesus Christ through faith. There is nothing we can ever do or fail to do to lose God's love. God will love us no matter what we do or do not do. This sounds fantastical, no, because it is not – it is the truth.

Under Grace, God's love for us does not change. Indeed, those who argue against Grace do like to qualify God's love for us. It may be a shock to some that they cannot sin enough to cause God to hate them; He will not. He will love them no matter how far away from Him they turn.

He will love you regardless of your weaknesses or shortcomings. His love for you is etched in stone; it is permanent and unconditional. "In Christ," nothing separates us from God's love. We have won even when we haven't fought or participated in the contest. Grace has made us more than conquerors, and everything is ours.

> "Ours," says Jesus, God is ours
> The Father, in Heaven, is ours
> The things He made are all ours
> The blessings and favors are ours

So, when we pray, we demand for ours
When we give thanks, we receive ours.

11 | TEN BENEFITS OF GRACE

1. Grace Makes Us Holy

"For the grace of God has appeared, bringing salvation to all men. It instructs us to renounce ungodliness and worldly passions, and to live sensible, upright, and godly lives in the present age."[466]

2. Grace Brings Us Salvation

"For the grace of God has appeared, bringing salvation to all men."[467]

"For it is by grace you have been saved, through faith--and this is not from yourselves, it is the gift of God."[468]

3. Grace Brings Healing

"Or with these surpassingly great revelations. So, to keep me from becoming conceited, I was given a thorn in my flesh, a messenger of Satan, to torment me. 8Three times I pleaded with the Lord to take it away from me. But He said to me, 'My

---

[466] Titus 2:11-12
[467] Titus 2:11
[468] Ephesians 2:8

grace is sufficient for you, for My power is perfected in weakness.' Therefore, I will boast all the more gladly in my weaknesses, so that the power of Christ may rest on me. For when I am weak, then I am strong …"[469]

4. Grace Makes Us Rich

"For you know the grace of our Lord Jesus Christ, that though he was rich, yet for your sake he became poor, so that you through his poverty might become rich."[470]

5. Grace Makes Us Excellent

"And God is able to bless you abundantly, so that in all things at all times, having all that you need, you will abound in every good work."[471]

"But since you excel in everything--in faith, in speech, in knowledge, in complete earnestness and in the love, we have kindled in you --see that you also excel in this grace of giving."[472]

6. Grace Makes Us Strong

"That is why, for Christ's sake, I delight

---

[469] 2 Corinthians 12:7-10
[470] 2 Corinthians 8:9
[471] 2 Corinthians 9:8
[472] 2 Corinthians 8:7

in weaknesses, in insults, in hardships, in persecutions, in difficulties. For when I am weak, then I am strong."[473]

7. Grace Makes Us Successful

"...and to know the love of Christ that surpasses knowledge, that you may be filled with all the fullness of God. Now to Him who is able to do infinitely more than all we ask or imagine, according to His power that is at work within us, to Him be the glory in the church and in Christ Jesus throughout all generations, forever and ever. Amen."[474]

8. Grace is All We Need

"But He said to me, 'My grace is sufficient for you, for My power is perfected in weakness.' Therefore I will boast all the more gladly in my weaknesses, so that the power of Christ may rest on me. That is why, for the sake of Christ, I delight in weaknesses, in insults, in hardships, in persecutions, in difficulties. For when I am weak, then I am strong."[475]

9. Grace Turns Liabilities into Assets

"Not only so, but we[a] also glory in our sufferings, because we know that suffering

---

[473] 2 Corinthians 12:10
[474] Ephesians 3:19-21
[475] 2 Corinthians 12:9-10

produces perseverance; perseverance, character; and character, hope. And hope does not put us to shame, because God's love has been poured out into our hearts through the Holy Spirit, who has been given to us."[476]

10. Grace is Infinite

"For out of His fullness [the superabundance of His grace and truth] we have all received grace upon grace [spiritual blessing upon spiritual blessing, favor upon favor, and gift heaped upon gift]."[477]

In Summary

Under the Law, it was impossible to achieve righteousness. Sometimes an animal was killed so that its blood could appease God. But that kind of holiness was seasonal and short lived. Christ's blood has permanently made those who believe in Him holy. Grace has brought to us true salvation and has given to us eternal life. His Grace has brought to us good health, material wealth and earthly and divine excellence. When we are weak, by Grace, we become strong. Just when we think we are out and lost, Grace finds us and brings

---

[476] Romans 5:3-5
[477] John 1:16 (Amplified Bible)

us before the great and mighty God. When we do less, Grace does more. When we do nothing, Grace does everything. Our only active part is to believe and trust in Jesus Christ.

> Oh, grace, wonderful grace
> I win each time I don't race
> I rise each time I do fall
> When beaten, all the time I regain all.
> O grace, amazing is understatement,
> My portion, you're my abatement
> When I am weak, then I am strong,
> What's helpful to me, can't be wrong.

12 | GRACE AND DISCIPLINE

Grace in the Disciplinary Process

Under the Dispensation of Grace, the disciplinary process must be of Grace. First, it is important to note that Church discipline is not an act of arbitrariness, just like God does not endorse a unilateral execution of His justice. Scripture has established that God's method of justice is based on Due Process. Thus, "The Lord is not slow in regard to the promise, as certain count slowness, but is long-suffering to us, not counselling any to be lost but all to pass on to reformation."[478] The interpretation of "must" in, "For we *must* all stand before Christ to be judged. We will each receive whatever we deserve for the good or evil we have done in this earthly body," denotes that Due Process is a matter of fact, and not discretion. The idea of Due Process or Procedural Fairness is the fair treatment, through the normal judicial system, of those accused of committing offences. At its core, it accords those who have been accused or those with claims made against them, the right to be heard and to be heard by a

---

[478] Young's Literal Translation of 2 Peter 3:9

person or persons (judge or tribunal) who is or are not biased against their case. In law, there are two presumptions: First, that one is innocent until evidence tendered through a fair process establishes otherwise; and second, that everyone has the capacity to defend themselves until otherwise determined.

Law is an instrument of justice. In all religions and political systems, this is trite law. However, justice cannot be said to have been meted out without establishing the truth basis. Justice must be done only after finding the truth. It is, therefore, necessary to any judicial or quasi-judicial or ecclesiastical fact-finding process that truth, and truth alone, determines how one is judged. Without establishing the truth, innocent people may be punished while the guilty may get off scot-free. Even God, who is Omnificent and Omnific,[479] the Transcendental[480] One, the Immanent,[481] Omnipotent[482] and Omniscient[483] – all concepts which make Him infallible and without error – is unable to arbitrarily mete out justice without providing an avenue for suspects to be heard.

It is, therefore, wrong to conclude that someone has sinned merely because such a

---

[479] All-creating
[480] Divine, beyond reach
[481] Existing in all, inherent
[482] Unlimited in power; able to do anything
[483] Knows everything

person is perceived to have done something wrong. "Sin" is a legal term – for it is the breaking of the law.[484] Humans cannot accurately judge whether someone has broken a law or not, let alone a divine law. Scripture forbids people from judging others arbitrarily – "Do not judge, or you too will be judged."[485] The connotation here is that one commits a triable act immediately they judge another, which automatically triggers their own judgment. Again, justice is preserved, for the Scripture does not say, "Judge not or you will be condemned." By saying, "Judge not, that ye be not judged,"[486] the Scripture leaves out room for Procedural Fairness. The person who allegedly judged another is given an opportunity to defend themselves.

The avenue set in Scripture, and which resounds with the idea of Due Process or Procedural Fairness, is called conscience or self-judgment. And the principle is set in this wise: "But if we were more discerning with regard to ourselves, we would not come under such judgment."[487] This is not only a universal precept, but it is also the safest landing pad. It gives the power to a person to avoid coming under the judgment of the just God. Conscience is the umpire

---

[484] 1 John 3:4
[485] Matthew 7:1
[486] Rendition of Matthew 7:1 in the King James Bible
[487] 1 Corinthians 11:31

or referee. It alerts one when it judges they have done or are about to do something wrong. If the wrongful act has been completed, conscience gives way to confession. Confession guarantees our forgiveness, because God is both faithful and just: "If we [freely] admit that we have sinned and confess our sins, He is faithful and just [true to His own nature and promises], and will forgive our sins and cleanse us continually from all unrighteousness [our wrongdoing, everything not in conformity with His will and purpose]."[488] This, effectively, means that when we expose ourselves before God, He does not take advantage of us. Rather, He sympathizes with us and fulfills the promise of forgiving us. And here is how God guarantees that He will not subject us to an embarrassing exposure without Due Process: "That if our conscience condemns us, that God is greater than our conscience and knows all things."[489] First, God relegates the act of judgment to our own consciences (hearts). That is, we judge ourselves. If our judgment is correct, we confess before God and we are forgiven. That is done and it ends right there. And last, God moves us into conviction by the Holy Spirit because He knows us and everything: "And He, when He comes, will

---

[488] 1 John 1:9 (Amplified Bible)
[489] 1 John 3:20

convict the world about [the guilt of] sin [and the need for a Savior], and about righteousness, and about judgment."[490]

It is vital to note, and very importantly so, three things from the above. First, it is not the role of humans to judge each other. That role is given to the person's conscience and to God. Once one judges themselves correctly and confesses, God fulfills His bargain and forgives. Second, if God should judge, He will be impartial, unbiased and He will observe Due Process. And third, any person who judges another, must observe Due Process, just like God does. Those who are given the rare chance of judging others, must do so with fear and trembling,[491] because they all, like their brethren, are equally prone to fallibility.[492]

Natural Justice

God (Jesus) Himself will pass judgment after hearing evidence and submissions. No person should be punished before they are heard. This principle of Natural Justice exist even in nature: Customary law embraces it, and it is a silver lining that blooms across the common-law and civil law jurisdictions. Whether in Church or in the nation-state, people who are subjects of these realms

---

[490] John 16:8
[491] See Philippians 2:12
[492] See Hebrews 4:14-16, *infra*.

must have access to fair hearing before impartial decision-makers.

Alternative Dispute Resolution (ADR)

Both our Lord Jesus Christ and Apostle Paul endorse ADR as the mechanism for resolving ecclesiastical conflicts and disputes. Church leaders do not have the right to mete out justice unilaterally or arbitrarily. Our Lord proposes that conflicts should be handled first and foremost between the parties themselves. This is assuming that an individual has failed to deal with their own internal conflicts of sin and offence. If an individual has listened to their conscience and confessed, they could have settled the issue within themselves.

However, there is a difference if one's action or conduct offends another. Personal absolution may have been done and completed and peace restored, but the other offended individual may still need to be pacified for the restoration of the relation to occur. Our Lord provides the following injunction:

> If your brother sins against you, go and tell him his fault, between you and him alone. If he listens to you, you have gained your brother. But if he does not listen, take one or two others along with you, that every charge may be established by

> the evidence of two or three witnesses. If he refuses to listen to them, tell it to the church. And if he refuses to listen even to the church, let him be to you as a Gentile and a tax collector.[493]

Many legal systems have borrowed the ADR method of handling conflicts from this paradigm. It involves three steps (although if the first step succeeds, there is no need to go to the second and the third). The first mechanism is called **negotiation**: "If your brother sins against you, go and tell him his fault, between you and him alone. If he listens to you, you have gained your brother." This mechanism is preferred and brings the best results. It keeps the relationship viable and issues of privacy are preserved. In fact, conflicts settled through negotiation bring great joy and happiness to the parties involved. But this method depends on both sides agreeing or accepting or as the Bible puts it, "listen[ing]" to each other. There is no third-party involved in this process. If successful, relations may remain cordial.

However, if one of the parties refuses to listen, this should trigger another conflict solution mechanism called **mediation**. Under mediation, the parties may choose an impartial, non-decision-maker who will act as a mediator. The mediator is non-partisan

---

[493] Matthew 18:15-17

and their only important role is to facilitate the settlement of the conflicts. They may be transactional or transformative at times, but their primary role is to assist the parties to come to an agreement, understanding or mutual consent. Our Lord puts it this way: "But if he does not listen, take one or two others along with you, that every charge may be established by the evidence of two or three witnesses." In ecclesiastical mediation, the mediator or mediators may also act as witnesses. And two are suggested in this Scripture as the minimum; it could also be three witnesses.[494]

In many legal systems, once mediation fails, the matter may be referred to **arbitration** (the use of an independent paid arbitrator to settle a dispute) or litigation (trial). However, as indicated in Scripture, once mediation fails, a *Church-Mediated Dispute Resolution* (CMDR) process may be preferred. CMDR involves the Church in the dispute resolution process. It is not the role of one person in the Church to resolve such conflicts even if one is a member of the five-fold ministries (Apostle, Prophet, Evangelist, Pastor and Teacher).[495] These work in the ministry to edify (build up) the Body and not to disunite it.[496]

Implicit in the "Matthew 18:15-17" injunction is the fact that no single Church

---

[494] See Deuteronomy 19:15
[495] Ephesians 4:11-13
[496] *Ibid.*

leader can judge between or among the offending members. A group of elders seems to qualify for such a role.[497] And the Bible seems also to suggest the plurality of elders, not an elder.[498] This will demonstrate that in matters of Church discipline, singularity may not be a preferred model. A Church may appoint a committee of elders for such a task. When the said committee reaches and renders a decision, that decision may be construed as having been made by the Church.

Disciplinary Process

If negotiation, mediation and CMDR have been attempted and the processes bear no fruit, our Lord suggests this: "And if he refuses to listen even to the church, let him be to you as a Gentile and a tax collector." However, in reading the Bible, we should not overlook the milieu which establishes the context in which certain pronouncements were made. As an aside, we should also be aware of the audience; certain words were spoken quintessentially to the Jews, and others to the Church. In this regard, however, our Lord was speaking to what would be the New Testament Church. Hitherto, the Church had not been established. What is cogent is

---

[497] See 1Timothy 3:1-7 and Titus 1:6-9
[498] *Ibid.*

the fact that the Lord predicted the establishment of the Church and gave a principle guideline on how it would resolve its conflicts. And although predictive, these words were uttered during the Dispensation of Law. The ideals of the New Testament and the Grace Dispensation became due after the death and resurrection of our Lord. The prescriptions given by Apostle Paul are, therefore, very germane to the discussion of dispute resolution under Grace.

And we begin with the event at Corinth:

> It is actually reported that there is sexual immorality among you, and of a kind that is intolerable even among pagans: A man has his father's wife. And you are proud! Shouldn't you rather have been stricken with grief and have removed from your fellowship the man who did this? Although I am absent from you in body, I am present with you in spirit, and I have already pronounced judgment on the one who did this, just as if I were present. When you are assembled in the name of our Lord Jesus and I am with you in spirit, along with the power of the Lord Jesus, hand this man over to Satan for the destruction of the

> flesh, so that his spirit may be
> saved on the Day of the Lord.[499]

Here we find a man who had committed an abomination. Even in British common-law Family Law jurisprudence, incestuous offences are crimes. The law, generally, does not allow sexual unions for parties within prohibited degrees of relationship. And this does not matter if they may be related by blood (consanguinity) or by marriage (affinity). And such relationships as having sexual relations with one's parent (by blood or marriage) are prohibited even under common-law ethics. In Canada, incest is an indictable offence punishable by up to fourteen years in prison:

> Every one commits incest who, knowing that another person is by blood relationship his or her parent, child, brother, sister, grandparent or grandchild, as the case may be, has sexual intercourse with that person. Everyone who commits incest is guilty of an indictable offence and is liable to imprisonment for a term of not more than 14 years.[500]

---

[499] 1 Corinthians 5:1-5
[500] *Canadian Criminal Code* (R.S.C., 1985, c. C-46), s. 155(1)(2)

The equivalent section of the Zambian *Penal Code Act*, provides for twenty years' incarceration or life imprisonment, thus:

> Any male person who has carnal knowledge of a female person who is to that person's knowledge his grandmother, mother, sister, daughter, grand-daughter, aunt or niece commits a felony and is liable, upon conviction, for a term of not less than twenty years and may be liable to imprisonment for life. Any female person who has carnal knowledge of a male person who is to that person's knowledge her grand-father, father, brother, son, grand-son, uncle or nephew commits a felony and is liable, upon conviction, for a term of not less than twenty years and may be liable to imprisonment for life.[501]

But Paul gives a death sentence for those implicated in incest in the Church: "…hand this man over to Satan for the destruction of the flesh, so that his spirit may be saved on the Day of the Lord." It is important to note three critical trends here.

First, this rule in the Bible, only applied to an incestuous relationship. There is nowhere else in the Bible where it was

---

[501] *Penal Code Act*, Chapter 87 of the Laws of Zambia, sections 159 (1)(2)(3)

recommended to "hand" a believer over to Satan.[502]

Second, it should be noted that this rule was recommended by Paul – the Lord's own hand-picked Apostle. The elders at Corinth could choose to enforce it or not. But even here, Paul is making an allegation; "It is actually reported that there is sexual immorality among you, and of a kind that is intolerable even among pagans: A man has his father's wife." Paul has no first-hand evidence; he relies on speculations or conjecture or even hearsay.

And third, Paul bemoans the lackadaisical attitude of the elders at Corinth: "And you are proud! Shouldn't you rather have been stricken with grief and have removed from your fellowship the man who did this?" Here, again, Paul laments that, if proven that such a man actually did what has been reported, the elders at Corinth behaved totally ingloriously. Thus, Paul, is hit with a righteous anger.[503]

The unified attitude towards those who have allegedly sinned in the New Testament is Grace. And this has been exemplified by two verses of Scripture. The first one is: "But go and learn what this means: 'I desire

---

[502] There is a caveat in 1 Corinthians 11:30 for those who abuse the Holy Communion, but this does not rise to the level of involving Satan in the execution of believers.
[503] See Ephesians 4:26-27

mercy, not sacrifice.' For I have not come to call the righteous, but sinners"[504] and the second one is, "For judgment is without mercy to one who has shown no mercy. Mercy triumphs over judgment."[505] In these verses, Grace is reestablished in the treatment of those who may succumb to sin.

God now prefers Grace (mercy) over judgment (justice), and so should we. This is most eloquently stated by Paul in this manner: "Brothers and sisters, if someone is caught in a sin, you who live by the Spirit should restore that person gently. But watch yourselves, or you also may be tempted."[506] The word used here is "gently" or graciously. This is reiterated in "We who are strong have an obligation to bear with the failings of the weak, and not to please ourselves"[507] and "And we urge you, brothers, to admonish the unruly, encourage the fainthearted, help the weak, and be patient with everyone."[508] To "gently," add "patiently" – that is how Grace deals with the weak in the Church. It does not rush to judgment or discipline. It suffers long just like God is rich in mercy

---

[504] Matthew 9:13 and Hosea 6:6
[505] James 2:13
[506] Galatians 6:1
[507] Romans 15:1
[508] 1 Thessalonians 5:14

and compassion, He is also slow to anger, and He abounds in love.[509]

Grace is, indeed, the quintessential New Testament standard. All of us are fallen creatures. Even if some among us may be called Bishops, pastors or otherwise, we all remain frail, weak and prone to iniquity, and, therefore, we ought to treat each other with Grace:

> Therefore, since we have a great high priest who has passed through the heavens, Jesus the Son of God, let us hold firmly to what we profess. For we do not have a high priest who is unable to sympathize with our weaknesses, but we have one who was tempted in every way that we are, yet was without sin. Let us then approach the throne of grace with confidence, so that we may receive mercy and find grace to help us in our time of need.[510]

The key reason why our Lord Jesus Christ is more suitable to saving us, is because He is able to sympathize with our weaknesses. And we, similarly, should emulate and imitate our Lord – the Big Brother.[511]

---

[509] Psalm 103:8
[510] Hebrews 4:14-16
[511] Hebrews 2:11

In Summary

In disciplining our fellow brothers and sisters, we should not rush to judgment, but we should gently and patiently offer ourselves to God and then to His Grace that is able to help us in our times of need. Therefore, we should look not only to our own interests, but also to the interests of others,[512] and to the weak, we should become weak. We should become all things to all people so that by all possible means we might expose some to God's Grace through faith.

> Oh, grace, surely I was a victim of my own vanity
> Held tightly under the jaws of brazen guile, I was captured by iniquity;
> What changed me, was Thy tearful and rapturous grace
> Your gentle, patient rebuke, erased my presumptuous sin without a trace.

---

[512] Philippians 2:4

13 | GOVERNMENT, LAW AND GRACE

Let everyone be subject to the governing authorities, for there is no authority except that which God has established. The authorities that exist have been established by God. Consequently, whoever rebels against the authority is rebelling against what God has instituted, and those who do so will bring judgment on themselves. For rulers hold no terror for those who do right, but for those who do wrong. Do you want to be free from fear of the one in authority? Then do what is right and you will be commended. For the one in authority is God's servant for your good. But if you do wrong, be afraid, for rulers do not bear the sword for no reason. They are God's servants, agents of wrath to bring punishment on the wrongdoer. Therefore, it is necessary to submit to the authorities, not only because of possible punishment but also as a matter of conscience. This is also why you pay taxes, for the authorities are God's servants, who give their full time to governing. Give to everyone what you owe them: If you owe taxes, pay taxes; if revenue, then revenue; if respect, then respect; if honor, then honor.[513]

God governs His creation. There is no rule or government on earth in which He has no say. The reason is simple; God made everything and everything is His: "The earth is the LORD's, and everything in it, the world, and all who live in it,"[514] and everywhere God is, He institutes order. God never leaves anything to chance. From the very beginning after He had created the heavens and the earth, He provided the sun and the moon to rule the day and the night, respectively: "God made two great lights-- the greater light to govern the day and the lesser light to govern the night."[515] And then God charged humanity to rule or govern His affairs on earth: "Then God said, 'Let Us make man in Our image, after Our likeness, to rule over the fish of the sea and the birds of the air, over the livestock, and over all the earth itself and every creature that crawls upon it.'"[516]

First, man's dominion on earth is total: The whole world and everything in it. It is

---

[513] Romans 13:1-7
[514] Psalm 24:1
[515] Genesis 1:16
[516] Genesis 1:25

delegated authority that man possesses on earth. In other words, man governs on behalf of God. Government was instituted on earth by God.

Second, man's dominion on earth is universal: Everywhere there is flora and fauna, man's authority is extended there. There is no place on earth where man's authority is limited.

And third, man's dominion on earth is legitimate: Man has real authority on earth. He did not acquire it by trickery like Satan did his, and neither was it given to him without law. In Ecclesiastes 3:1 we read, "For everything there is a season, and a time for every matter under Heaven ."[517] And this is also expressly stated in Daniel: "He changes times and seasons; he removes kings and sets up kings; he gives wisdom to the wise and knowledge to those who have understanding."[518] And this is to be the order for as long as Heaven and earth shall remain: "While the earth remains, seedtime and harvest, cold and heat, summer and winter, day and night, [and government] shall not cease."[519]

Every nation, tribe, race and peoples on earth are governed. This is because government is a divine institution; it has never been a man-made experiment. And as far as God is concerned, there is no divinely

---

[517] See also Genesis 1:14-19
[518] Daniel 2:21
[519] Genesis 8:22 (emphasis added)

stipulated method of governing. Each part of the world, and, indeed, each nation or people, has the freewill to adopt any form of government it considers appropriate.

There is, however, implied in the Bible, the consent of the governed: "For there is no respect of persons with God."[520] With God, all people are equal. And each member of society should have an equal voice in the governing affairs of their lands. And once an organized set of people agree (by appointment or vote) on a type of government they want, God in Heaven also agrees with them.

The way a government is formed means very little to God. However, every good government must be founded on four divinely sanctioned principles or values: Righteousness, justice, truth and morality.

Ultimate Role of Government

The end product of any government is to ensure prosperity and peace for its people. This is what is partly referred to in the passage above as "…authority is God's servant for your good."

And in another verse, the Bible encourages us to pray for those in authority so that "… a quiet and peaceable life we may lead in all piety and gravity."[521] The

---

[520] Romans 2:11
[521] 1 Timothy 2:2

combination of these two verses highlight the following:

First, that the ultimate end of living under a government is so that we can revere (worship) God and be pure (holy) before Him. This is the transcendental goal of the entire creation. When this present world passes away and another one in perpetuity comes, we shall all be under God's government. We shall be preoccupied with worshipping Him while remaining perpetually pure before Him. This is the greatest mystery of the entire philosophy of good and bad, now and future and death and life. This is the hope all humanity live with or must live with. We shall not just expire and there will be nothing; no, we live with the hope of resurrection. We believe that God's Kingdom will be established first in our hearts, and then in perpetuity here on earth. In that Kingdom, God Himself shall be our light and source of our peace and prosperity.

But then, second, and this applies to here and now, the purpose of government is to bring happiness to the peoples by way of enabling prosperity and peace in the land. People are happy when they have their ends met and they live in peace.[522] Prosperity alone without peace is thuggery; and peace without prosperity is drudgery. Both are required to create a nation of

---

[522] See Jeremiah 29:7 and 1 Timothy 2:2

happy people. And every government must strive to bring prosperity within its borders while preserving peace and harmony among its people internally and with neighbors externally.

Four Core Values of Government

The first two co-equal core values of governing are righteousness and justice: "Righteousness and justice are the foundation of your throne; steadfast love and faithfulness go before you."[523] Imagine a house built on the foundation of rightness and fairness. This means that all things proceed from there. Decisions, plans, policies and legislation. The Bible warns: "Do not twist justice in legal matters by favoring the poor or being partial to the rich and powerful. Always judge people fairly."[524] The guiding principles for establishing a government where people will prosper and live in peace and be happy are these two.

This means that not only will the affairs of the nation be conducted in the spirit of fairness and rightness, but also that the governors will be men and women who desire to rule fairly and righteously. Such leaders will give equal gravitas to the plight of every citizen without harassment or

---

[523] Psalm 89:14
[524] Leviticus 19:15

discrimination. Moreover, such leaders will likely be corrupt-free, hard working and dutiful.

The last set of principles which are desired for government are truth and morality.

The idea of truth and government is an especially essential part of leadership. The central tenet of truth is that it does not only bring freedom, but it also establishes it: "So Jesus said to the Jews who had believed in him, 'If you abide in my word, you are truly my disciples, and you will know the truth, and the truth will set you free.'"[525] Truth and words walk side by side.

First, truth in itself empowers nations to be free. When people know the truth, they are at liberty to make informed decisions. When leaders are credible, it liberates the citizens. Truth breeds transparency and makes both those who are governed and the governors accountable.

But second, truth establishes trust in the government. People tend to believe in leaders who are truthful and who are accountable to their words. In nations where lies rule, people easily lose trust in their own systems and structures. They do not trust their leaders, either. This is because truth is the basis of trust. And a people will find it difficult to trust

---

[525] John 8:31-32

governors who do not keep their words or promises.

The Bible says, "Righteousness exalteth a nation, and the goodliness of peoples is a sin-offering."[526] And as indicated above, "For the authorities do not strike fear in people who are doing right, but in those who are doing wrong. Would you like to live without fear of the authorities? Do what is right, and they will honor you."[527] Morality is knowing right from wrong. One of the reasons why government exists is to protect right and punish wrong or evil. Right or "goodliness" or even loveliness or goodness is a value that must be harnessed. The Bible is on point when it states, "A voice was saying, 'Cry out!' Another said, 'What should I cry out?' All humanity is grass, and all its goodness is like the flower of the field."[528]

Indeed, all humanity has fading beauty – unless it is tendered, it will easily wither away. The rightfulness of people ought not to be left to chance; it must be tendered. The frailty and faultiness of the people, similarly, should be managed. Good or right ought to be enforced and not left to the whims of every citizen.

Rightness brings dignity and respect to a nation but immorality is a disgrace to any

---

[526] Proverbs 14:34 (Young's Literal Translation)
[527] Romans 13:3
[528] Isaiah 40:6 (Holman Christian Standard Bible)

people on the face of the globe.[529] There is no nation that, knowingly, intentionally, purposely or deliberately, encourages its people to do bad things. Such a government will be ostracized by the community of nations and will be unpopular in the eyes of God.

Law and Core Values

Law is the vehicle through which a government transacts righteousness, justice, truth and morality leading to peaceful existence and prosperity. The happiest people on earth also enjoy good laws that shield and empower them. Bad laws dictate, good laws inspire.

The entire Scripture (Old and New Testaments) train us in righteousness: "All Scripture is God-breathed and is useful for teaching, rebuking, correcting and training in righteousness."[530] And law, in general, codifies or pronounces those principles societies consider right. Without law, people would do anything even if it was harmful to them and to others. It is the role of government to enforce good laws so that people do not do whatever they think or feel is right: "In those days Israel had no king; all the people did whatever seemed

---

[529] Proverbs 14:34, *supra*.
[530] 2 Timothy 3:16

right in their own eyes."[531] Such a society would likely breed anarchy.

Leaders must be chosen with understanding and deliberation so that they cannot only enact good and effective laws, but also that they can be committed to enforcing them fairly and without discrimination. That is the reason why the Bible encourages nations to choose wise, well-informed and respectable people to be in government: "Choose for yourselves wise, understanding, and respected men from each of your tribes, and I will appoint them as your leaders."[532]

Implicit in this verse is the versatility of leaders elected or appointed. Good leaders do not just enact just laws, but they engender progressively just and innovative ideas in government.

"Development" and "civilization" are the brainchildren of brilliant ideas from both the governors and the governed. Nations do not "develop" by accident; they develop because diligent governments enact laws that motivate citizens to breed good and enlightened ideas.

Similarly, a nomenclature most vocal in the delineation of the so-called free societies and the so-called authoritarian is the word "civilized," from which civilization is derived. Civilized societies are

---

[531] Judges 21:25
[532] Deuteronomy 1:13

simply "civil" societies, in the sense that they are cultured, enlightened, polite and adherents to their citizens' dignity and respect for human rights. At the heart of civility is morality, ethics, justice, righteousness and goodness. Good laws are integral to people's civility. And it is in order to suggest that just laws can only be enacted by just men and women; men and women of integrity.

The Bible instructs: "Learn to do good; seek ye justice, correct oppression; bring justice to the fatherless, and plead the widow's cause,"[533] and "He has told you, O man, what is good; and what does the Lord require of you but to do justice, and to love kindness, and to walk humbly with your God?"[534] God does not just instruct us to seek and bring justice, but He (God) loves justice: "The Lord is righteous, he loves justice."[535]

Truth is inherent in all laws – divine and temporal. God's law is truth: "Thy righteousness *is* an everlasting righteousness, and thy law *is* the truth."[536] God's law came from God who is truth itself, so, it was expected to be true. As discussed, truth lends authenticity to just ideals and is essential to a trusting relationship between the governors and the

---

[533] Isaiah 1:17
[534] Micah 6:8
[535] Psalms 11:7
[536] Psalm 119:142

governed. If God's law were not true, it would be impossible to believe Him or in Him. We trust that whatever God has said in His law (God's Word) is true and that is the reason why we have confidence in Him and we trust Him.

Similarly, we expect our governments to have system of enactment of statutes or of reaching court decisions that are clear, fair and transparent. We expect that our national laws will have been well-thought-through, widely researched and reasoned and are relevant to our existence here on earth. Otherwise, we would not be obeying them.

James advises, "So whoever knows the right thing to do and fails to do it, for him it is sin."[537] Two things are implied in this verse. First, it is that someone has been schooled in the knowledge of right. Only those who know right can be guilty of not doing it. And the last assumption is that wrong or evil is defined by law. Without law, it would be difficult to separate right from wrong. It is no wonder we have argued in this book that Law introduced sin and gave it its strength. However, with the same token, without law in general, we would not appreciate right or shun evil.

---

[537] James 4:17

Grace and Core Values

This last point above leads us to the importance of Grace as presented in the New Testament. Law, notwithstanding, God's preference for humanity is Grace. He has stated very eloquently in this fashion: "To do righteousness and justice is more desirable to the LORD than sacrifice."[538] We have already submitted that God's righteousness has been imputed on us by Grace through faith:

> And therefore it was imputed to him for righteousness. Now it was not written for his sake alone, that it was imputed to him; but for us also, to whom it shall be imputed, if we believe on him that raised up Jesus our Lord from the dead; who was delivered for our offences, and was raised again for our justification.[539]

Without obeying a single law, but only by trusting God and acting in faith, Abraham was declared right before God. God credited to him righteousness just on account of his faith. Under Grace, faith in God makes us righteous.

---

[538] Proverbs 21:3
[539] Romans 4:22-25

It may be argued that Grace is enforceable by God because God has the patience and character to do so. However, human governments may be at odds or even at a loss to rule by Grace. Indeed, governments of the civilized societies have elected to be ruled by laws rather than by men.

Granted. But wouldn't it be easier to live in societies where there are no laws at all? No-one would be indebted to another on account of an omission or commission of a wrong. We would be each other's keepers.[540] We would not do to others what we would not like done to us.[541] And we would owe others nothing except to love them. Indeed, if we loved others wholeheartedly, we would need no law to obey:

> Owe no man anything, but to love one another, for he that loveth another hath fulfilled the law. For this, "Thou shalt not commit adultery," "Thou shalt not kill," "Thou shalt not steal," "Thou shalt not bear false witness," "Thou shalt not covet," and if there be any other commandment, all are briefly comprehended in this saying, namely: "Thou shalt love thy neighbor as thyself." Love

---

[540] See Genesis 4:9
[541] See Leviticus 19:18 and Matthew 7:12

worketh no ill to his neighbor; therefore love is the fulfillment of the law.[542]

The reason why we need laws in human societies is because we cannot love each other unconditionally. Sometimes, we choose not to love one another. Because of selfishness, greed and love for self, we are unable to live without laws.

The law would be irrelevant if we lived, say, by the Golden Rule code. And if we loved God and our neighbors as ourselves, there would be no need for law. This is because love is the fulfilment of the law.

Until we reach "love-immunity" in human societies, we will still need the letter of the law to manage peace, prosperity and happiness. However, we still rejoice because God is ahead of the game; for the world to be, He is on time acclimatizing us to how things should and will be. In this Dispensation of Grace and in New Jerusalem,[543] we will not need any laws at all; we will live in perpetuity in the atmosphere of love.

Despite the forgone, it is imperative to note that the values of righteousness, justice, truth and morality are germane in the governing affairs of human societies, even here and now in the Dispensation of

---

[542] Romans 13:8-10
[543] Revelation 3:12 and Revelation 21:2

Grace. For one, leaders and those who enforce human laws, should temper judgment with mercy: "There will be no mercy for those who have not shown mercy to others. Mercy triumphs over judgment."[544]

Grace compels us to regard the humanity of our fellow human beings even when they have offended us and the law. Jesus, for example, proscribed an eye for an eye or revenge: "You have heard that it was said, 'Eye for eye and tooth for tooth.' But I tell you not to resist an evil person. If someone slaps you on your right cheek, turn to him the other also."[545]

In the same way Jesus instructs us to prefer reconciliation to litigation: "Settle matters quickly with your adversary who is taking you to court. Do it while you are still together on the way, or your adversary may hand you over to the judge, and the judge may hand you over to the officer, and you may be thrown into prison."[546] In other words, our Lord is suggesting that we prefer non-legal methods of dispute resolution to legal means. Many nations have caught up to this mechanism, many nations of the world are preferring Alternative Dispute Resolution (ADR) to litigation or adjudication. Our Lord provides the reasons why ADR may be preferable to

---

[544] James 2:13
[545] Matthew 5:38 - 39
[546] Matthew 5:25

law-sanctioned methods of solving or resolving conflicts or disputes: "Settle matters quickly," i.e., it is efficient; "…while you are still together on the way," i.e., it preserves relationships; and "…you may be thrown into prison," i.e., it may prevent incarceration. ADR is more akin to Grace than to Law.

Under Grace, justice is preferred to revenge. And this is the same reason why truly Christian nations or nations whose constitutions are founded on the supremacy of God should not allow the death penalty.

Under Grace, governments should enforce the law justly while at the same time realizing that they are weak themselves. In other words, the law must be enforced in humility and with justice: "He has shown you, O mortal, what is good. And what does the LORD require of you? To act justly and to love mercy and to walk humbly with your God."[547]

Governments should realize that they represent God and must act as God would in every circumstance. And this might mean injecting aspects of social justice in adjudication, such as providing alternatives to imprisonment, and applying the principles of sentencing fairly and not arbitrarily. If possible, governments should be proactive in inculcating a culture of love, tolerance, dignity and respect in its citizens

---

[547] Micah 6:8

through education, activism, lobby, entertainment or religion. It defeats the purpose for irresponsible governments to allow behaviors and tendencies which have as their intrinsic character the demeaning, disrespecting or degrading of other human beings.

In Summary

Governing people who are under Grace should be, comparatively, less strenuous than those under Law. This is because of two qualities that are implied in our passage of Scripture above,[548] namely, a lively conscience and self-control: "Therefore, it is necessary to submit to the authorities, not only because of possible punishment but also as a matter of conscience."[549]

Those who are filled with the Holy Spirit under Grace should allow their consciences to guide them. As long as the laws enacted by legislatures or decided by the courts are good and fair, live consciences will dictate good responses even without threats of sanction or punishment. And to crown it all, Grace is a valuable partner to governments on earth, because it is our newest schoolmaster training us how to live worthy, self-controlled and productive lives as we await the New Jerusalem: "For the

---

[548] See Romans 13:1-7, *supra*.
[549] Romans 13:5, *supra*.

LAW & GRACE

grace of God has appeared, bringing salvation for all people. And we are instructed to turn from godless living and sinful pleasures. We should live in this evil world with wisdom, righteousness, and devotion to God, awaiting and confidently expecting the [fulfillment of our] blessed hope and the glorious appearing of our great God and Savior, Christ Jesus."[550]

> O God, I have no words, no capacity
> How can I comprehend this wonder?
> Your grace is supremely of felicity
> What it's done, goes way yonder.

---

[550] Titus 2:11-13 (Amplified Bible)

ABOUT THE AUTHOR

Charles Mwewa (LLB. BA. Edu. + Engl., BA. Legal Studies. Cert. Law. DIBM. LLM.) is a Dad, author, and poet. Mwewa is the author of over 50 books and counting in all genres – fiction (novels), non-fiction and poetry. Mwewa, his wife, and their three girls, reside in the Capital City of Ottawa, Canada

Websites:
charlesmwewa.com
acpress.ca

Facebook:
https://www.facebook.com/authorcharlesmwewa

Email:
info@acpress.ca

Amazon

Online access to this book:
www.amazon.com/dp/1988251427

INDEX

A

a Will, 98, 105
Aaron, 158, 159
Abraham, 108, 109, 110, 119, 147, 155, 191, 195
Abrahamic Covenant, 97
Abram, 23, 155, 167, 176, 196
absolution, 189, 234
abundance, 86, 133, 152, 155, 163, 164, 189, 196, 200, 201
accruals, 95, 105
Achaia, 199, 205
acquitted, 104
Acts, 2, 84, 86, 107, 117, 123, 125, 126, 129, 132, 161, 177, 190, 197, 205
Adamic, 105
adjudication, 3, 260, 261
administrator, 99
ADR, 234, 235, 260
adultery, 11, 33, 63
adversary, 62, 260
affinity, 239
Africa, 34
Alternative Dispute Resolution, 260
Amaziah, 152
ambassador, 59
Amen, 133, 150, 176, 212, 225
Americans, 34
anarchy, 15, 254
angels, 39, 73, 112, 122, 147
Apostle, 20, 49, 73, 119, 129, 181, 213, 220, 234, 236, 238, 241
appearance, 68, 72, 73, 112, 149, 218
arbitration, 236
assumption, 11, 28, 206, 256
atonement, 72
atoning sacrifice, 76
attestation, 102, 140, 194

B

Baal, 42
Balaam, 119
bank account, 83
Bashan, 114
beauty, 72, 74, 83, 115, 148, 169
behavior, xxi, 1, 4, 127, 145
beneficiaries, 97, 101
Bible, xi, xvii, xix, 4, 6, 7, 13, 21, 35, 68, 129, 134, 167, 168, 183, 188, 191, 217, 226, 231, 235, 237,

240, 248, 250, 252, 254, 255, 263
birth, xix, xxii, 73, 142
Bishops, 243
blood of Christ, 78
Book of Life, xxiv
Book of the Law', 176
British, 239
Buddhists, 8
bulls, 114
business, 137, 177, 178, 188
by-laws, 208

C

Calvary, 112
Canaanite, 150
Canada, 239
Canon Law, 8
caselaw, 2
Catholic Church, 8
celebration, 209
Ceremonial Law, 8, 12, 14
ceremonies, 45
Charismatic, 8
charitable organizations, 177
cheerful giver, 180, 200
Christian law, 8
Christianity, 8, 9, 157
church, 118, 119, 170, 172, 175, 177, 178, 194, 196, 197, 199, 202, 206, 207, 208, 225
Church-Mediated Dispute Resolution, 236
circumcised, 41
civil codes, 3
CMDR, 236, 237
Codex Hammurabi, 12, 14, 15
common-law, 2
community, 13, 253
compassion, 53, 61
compulsion, 179, 180, 200, 202, 204
condemn, xxii, 29, 34, 36, 39, 64, 66, 118
condemnation, 36, 67, 104, 115, 220
confess, xxiii, 31, 58, 60, 117, 118, 121
confidence, 29, 35, 47, 118, 133, 199, 219
conflicts, 261
congregations, 172, 174, 204
consanguinity, 239
conscience, xxii, 27, 29, 31, 33, 34, 35, 40, 78
consent, 236, 248
Corinth, 238, 241
Cornelius, 129
courts, 2, 4
Creationist Theory, 173
Creator, 67, 111, 113, 167, 190
criminal law, 3, 12
cross, 71, 72, 83, 112, 143, 219
crucifixion, 105

culture, xxii, 121, 175
cummin, 192
curse, 21, 121, 158, 171, 176, 183
customary, 1
Customary law, 55, 233

D

David, 85, 131, 142, 143, 145
death, xvii, xx, 16, 25, 26, 53, 56, 60, 64, 65, 66, 67, 72, 76, 79, 100, 101, 104, 106, 111, 112, 114, 116, 118, 121, 122, 123, 126, 129, 142, 144, 185, 219, 220, 238, 240, 249, 261
death penalty, 261
death sentence, 101, 240
debts, 102
decalogue, xix
decision-maker, 235
decrees, 6, 7
democratic body, 2
Deuteronomy, 12, 13, 14, 152, 162, 176, 216
devil, 36, 39, 112, 122, 166
devourer, 163, 164, 165, 166, 169
Dinah, 143
disciples, 74, 193, 201, 213
disciplinary process, 229
discipline, 37, 229, 237, 242
discrimination, 251, 254

Dispensation of Grace, 171, 190, 193, 209, 211, 212, 217
Dispensation of Law, 192
disputes, 234, 261
divine institution, 247
Divine Law, 8, 9
doctrine, 2, 176
doctrines, 100
dominion, 111, 246, 247
donkey, 11, 119
Due Process, 229, 231, 233

E

Early Church, 181
ecclesiastical conflicts, 234
ecclesiastical law, 8, 208
education, 125
Egypt, 9, 144
elders, 5, 177, 237, 241
elements, 96
embarrassing, 232
employment standards, 206
enemies, 5, 74, 155, 167, 182
England, 2, 4, 9
enjoyment, 51, 173
enlightened, 42
enrichment, 189
entertainment, 262
Esau, 145
estate, 53, 55, 99, 100, 101, 170
Esther, 85, 147

eternal life, 19, 104, 114, 174, 226
Evangelical, 8
Evangelist, 236
evidence, 64, 66, 168, 174, 230, 233, 235, 236, 241
excellence, 20, 182, 226
excellent, 51, 148
executor, 100
Exodus, 11, 13, 14, 141

F

fairness, 250
faith, xxiii, xxiv, 17, 20, 21, 22, 23, 24, 25, 26, 38, 40, 45, 49, 51, 59, 60, 68, 70, 74, 75, 76, 83, 85, 108, 109, 110, 115, 116, 117, 130, 131, 132, 134, 149, 169, 171, 172, 175, 182, 191, 192, 212, 214, 220, 223, 224
faithful, 36, 58, 72, 84, 104, 134, 188, 232
faithfulness, 4, 73, 144, 152
fallibility, 233
falling from grace, 40
Family Law, 97, 239
famine, 53, 204, 205
Father, xxiv, 36, 39, 40, 46, 53, 54, 57, 61, 69, 70, 71, 73, 76, 81, 112, 114, 119, 122, 126, 130, 150, 182, 208, 210, 216, 217, 220, 221
favoritism, 129
fear and trembling, 233
feasts, 187
feet, 5, 54, 61, 74, 115, 161
fellowship, 38, 61, 123, 238, 241
financial support, 175, 205
five senses, 96
five-fold ministries, 236
flock, 140, 156, 157, 162, 220
flora and fauna, 190, 247
food, 34, 53, 56, 74, 149, 155, 163, 164, 178, 203
fool, 49, 50, 184
foreigner, 10, 162
forgiveness, 40, 58, 60, 61, 62, 67, 110, 120
fraud, 137
freedom, xxi, xxii, xxiii, 28, 35, 109, 115, 116, 134, 217
freeman, 15
freewill, 161, 248
fruit, 124, 156, 163, 164, 166, 172
fruitfulness, 97, 164

G

Garden of Eden, xvii
Genesis, xvii, 13, 23, 30, 143, 144, 145, 146, 147, 150, 152, 155, 167, 196,

210
genius, 50
Gentiles, 85, 107, 109, 125, 129, 131, 133, 205
gifts, 86, 122, 173, 175, 197, 199, 212, 213, 215, 216, 217
glory, xix, 20, 46, 66, 70, 71, 72, 73, 74, 79, 81, 83, 113, 114, 127, 130, 135, 136, 150, 184, 186, 212, 214, 215, 225
God's Word, 214, 256
God-made law, 9
Golden Rule, xxi
Good News, 42, 85, 122
Gospel, 21, 42, 107, 115, 116, 117, 118, 120, 121, 122, 124, 126, 129, 130, 131, 202, 203, 204, 205, 206
governed, xxi, 247, 248, 251, 256
government, 1, 246, 247, 248, 249, 250, 251, 252, 253
governors, 250, 251, 255
Grace Dispensation, 200
Grace of God, 110, 126, 133, 136, 174
Greatest Commandment, 35
Greek, 19, 21, 212
guarantor, 100
guardian, 17, 108, 109
guidelines, xxiv, 4, 12, 206, 208

H

happiness, 211, 235, 249, 259
healing the sick, 74
hearsay, 241
Heaven, 24, 52, 59, 71, 82
Hebrew, 13, 19, 21, 173, 211
heirs, 83, 99
Hell, 24, 33, 39, 113, 117, 121
heresy, 171
heretic, 168, 171
High Priest, 159
Hindus, 8
holiness, 32, 68, 85, 110, 131, 150, 226
Holy of Holies, 30, 160
Holy Place, 160
Holy Spirit, 38, 39, 42, 43, 49, 52, 81, 98, 99, 105, 196, 226, 262
homicide, xviii
honor, 144, 146, 151, 171, 172
human agent, 39, 74, 196, 216
humble, 86, 134, 139
humility, 40, 112, 134, 199, 261
hypocrites, 74, 192, 211

I

Immanent, 230
immoral, xix, 124
immorality, 37, 238, 241, 252
immortals, 95
impossible, xix, xxii, xxiii, 24, 42, 160, 226
imprisonment, 3, 239, 240, 261
imputation, 70, 188
in Christ, 20, 21, 24, 25, 33, 36, 46, 52, 58, 68, 69, 71, 72, 74, 81, 83, 85, 109, 110, 115, 116, 132, 134, 136, 149, 168, 182, 214, 215, 217, 218, 225
incarceration, 261
incarnation, 112
incest, 239, 240
infallible, 230
inheritance, 55, 56, 80, 81, 83, 95, 99, 100, 101, 120, 158, 159, 161, 197
iniquity, xix, 159
injunction, xxi, 14, 234, 236
inspiration, 46
instructor, 68
intercedes, 69
intercessory work, 105
interventions, 95
intestate, 98
Isaac, 151
Israel, 9, 11, 115, 129, 144, 152, 156, 157, 158, 159, 160, 162, 171, 211

J

Jacob, 144, 145, 155, 159, 167
Jerusalem, 82, 150, 181, 205
Jesus Christ, xxi, xxii, xxiii, 21, 23, 26, 31, 32, 66, 68, 69, 70, 73, 75, 77, 81, 85, 86, 116, 117, 118, 123, 124, 129, 130, 131, 133, 136, 150, 153, 172, 178, 182, 186, 187, 212, 217, 218, 219, 224, 227
Jews, 24, 79, 107, 108, 109, 129, 130, 133
Joab, 146
Jonathan, 142, 145
Joseph, 142, 144, 145, 147, 161
joy, 6, 46, 113, 114, 235
Judaism, 13, 14, 157
judgment, 37, 38, 39, 66, 137, 245, 260
judgments, 7, 18
jurisprudence, 97, 239
justice, 111, 192, 248, 250, 253, 255, 257, 259, 261
justification, 75, 76, 122

K

kindness, 144, 147, 255
Kingdom, 25, 76, 79, 99, 105, 202, 249
Kingdom of God, 25, 76, 79, 202
Kingdom, God, 249
kings, 74
knowledge of God, 20, 21, 29, 35, 86, 133, 138
knowledge of good and evil, xvii, 30
Kohens, 159

L

labor, 10, 45, 84, 85, 134, 135, 166, 198, 207
Lamb, xxiv
Law and Grace, 63, 186
Law Period, 155, 156, 163, 173, 196
laziness, 188
leaders, 194, 196, 197, 202, 250, 251, 254, 260
legislation, 250
legislature, 2
leprosy, 193
letters of administration, 100
Levi, 158, 159, 160, 195
Levites, 157, 159, 160, 161, 163, 165, 168, 195
Leviticus, 13, 14, 156, 172
liabilities, 102
lions, 114
litigation, 236, 260
liturgies, 125
logic, 51, 215
Lot, 147
love, xxi, 5, 6, 10, 17, 31, 34, 35, 39, 40, 41, 44, 45, 47, 53, 56, 57, 60, 69, 71, 73, 77, 84, 107, 114, 121, 123, 132, 134, 135, 140, 152, 153, 167, 169, 182, 183, 184, 192, 199, 208, 209, 213, 214, 224, 225
love-immunity, 259

M

Macedonia, 198, 205
majesty, 72, 140
mammon, 188
marriage, 151
master planner, 98
material prosperity, 164
material richness, 136
meat, 166
mediation, 235, 236
mediator, 62, 120, 235
Melchizedek, 155, 167, 176, 195, 196
Mephibosheth, 145
mercy, 47, 55, 56, 66, 67, 101, 133, 148, 192, 194, 219, 242, 243, 260, 261

methodologies, 96, 169
milk, 166
minds, xxii, 12, 29, 31
mint, 192
misdeeds, 104
miserable, 79
money, 83, 122, 124, 137, 161, 182, 187, 198, 199, 202, 203, 204, 219
moral, xix, 1, 3, 8, 172, 183, 189, 208, 216
Moral Law, 4, 7, 8, 9, 15
morality, 3, 8, 189, 248, 251, 253, 259
Morality, 3, 252
Mosaic Law, 8, 9, 13, 22, 64, 65, 67, 167, 176, 193, 200
Moses, xxi, 9, 12, 13, 23, 25, 30, 31, 63, 64, 65, 73, 74, 141, 155, 156, 163, 187, 191, 193, 198, 219
motivation, 46, 121
mountains, 115
movie theater, 34
murder, xviii, xxi, 11, 57
Muslims, 8

N

nation-state, 233
Natural Justice, 233
negotiation, 235
neighbors, 250, 259
New Jerusalem, 83, 259, 262

New Testament, 21, 22, 139, 153, 161, 168, 170, 171, 172, 175, 177, 179, 181, 189, 190, 191, 192, 194, 196, 200, 202, 204, 205, 206, 207, 208, 210, 211, 213, 217, 219
Noah, 145
North American Christians, 34
Numbers, 13, 119, 143, 161

O

obedience, 78, 85, 104, 131, 163, 164, 171, 172, 182, 186, 189, 191
observations, 12
Old Covenant, 164, 168, 173, 174, 175, 194
Old Testament, 9, 13, 18, 139, 140, 141, 142, 145, 148, 166, 170, 176, 189, 191, 192, 194, 195, 209, 210, 217
Omnific, 230
Omnificent, 230
Omnipotent, 230
Omniscient, 230
Only Begotten Son, 74
oppression, 255
ordinances, 8

P

pagans, 37, 162, 238, 241
pardons, 66, 67
Parliament, 2
Pastor, 236
Patriarchal Period, 167
Paul, 2, 20, 21, 22, 48, 49, 68, 72, 85, 119, 121, 126, 131, 135, 177, 181, 182, 186, 197, 198, 199, 200, 201, 202, 203, 205, 212, 213
Pauline Theology, 180, 182
pay tithe, 192
peace, xxiii, 20, 31, 32, 65, 86, 115, 129, 133, 214
penalty, xvii, xix, 76
Pentecostal, 8
perfection, 5, 17, 75, 77, 79, 175
Pharaoh, 146, 147
Pharisees, 63, 65, 71, 192, 194
philanthropy, 205
pleasure, 42, 47, 127, 220
policies, 208, 250
policy, 203, 206
political systems, 230
portion, 13, 158, 159, 160, 171, 181, 227
post-Law, 176
Potiphar, 147
poverty, 55, 136, 187, 201, 218, 224
power, 20, 21, 38, 40, 50, 60, 61, 66, 67, 71, 72, 74, 84, 85, 111, 120, 126, 131, 132, 135, 136, 150, 152, 175, 185, 186, 189, 212, 215, 224, 225
praiseworthy, 52
prayer, 198, 207, 209, 210, 214, 220
preacher, 118, 119, 120, 121, 124, 171
preaching, 42, 57, 120, 126, 187, 198, 202, 203, 205, 207
precedent, 2
precepts, 5, 6, 7, 12, 14, 18
pre-Law, 167, 176
presence, 29, 46, 113, 133, 162, 217
presumptions, 230
priest, 72, 77, 155, 167, 193, 197
prison, 62, 260
privacy, 235
Procedural Fairness, 229, 231
Prodigal Son, 53, 57, 60, 61
prohibition, 24
promise, 6, 7, 11, 29, 109, 130, 144, 191
promises, 20, 169, 195, 252
promisor, 80, 97
pronouncements, 8, 237
prophet, 42, 205

Prophet, 144, 163, 236
Prophet Malachi, 163
prosperity, 171, 248, 249, 253, 259
prosperity ministries, 171
psychology, 121
punishment, xxi, 3, 12, 64, 67, 105, 111, 115, 117, 245, 262

Q

queens, 74

R

reconciliation, 58, 60, 61, 62
redemption, 31, 70, 81, 110, 120, 130, 134
regeneration, 29
regulations, 8, 18, 22, 172
relationships, 261
religion, 4, 8, 13, 153, 157
remedies, 11
restoration, 234
resurrection, xx, 81, 85, 99, 113, 131, 238, 249
revenge, 260, 261
revenues, 207
rewards, 11, 12, 17, 38, 66, 84
rich, 50, 51, 83, 136, 149, 150, 151, 173, 187, 189, 190, 201, 218, 224

righteous anger, 241
righteousness, xxi, xxii, xxiii, 17, 19, 23, 24, 25, 39, 59, 68, 70, 76, 77, 78, 80, 108, 109, 110, 111, 129, 130, 136, 140, 172, 187, 194, 213, 226
Romeo-Justinian-French, 2
Rule of Grace, 174, 175, 176, 179, 181, 186, 209

S

Sabbath, xxiii, 10
sacrifice, 23, 26, 103, 123, 150, 174, 183, 242, 257
sacrifices, 22, 84, 117, 161
salary, 175, 206, 207
Salem, 155, 167
salvation, xxiii, 24, 25, 27, 36, 40, 42, 44, 49, 57, 67, 78, 81, 85, 98, 104, 115, 117, 122, 124, 127, 132, 134, 223, 226, 263
Samaritan, 159
sanctions, xxi, 2, 11, 12
sanctuary, 141
Satan, 33, 38, 105, 110, 111, 112, 113, 136, 223, 238, 240, 241, 247
satisfaction, 52
Savior, 68, 126, 127
schoolmaster, 16, 108, 262
Scripture, xx, 85, 131, 172, 214

Second Coming, 69
seed, xxiii, 27, 29, 136, 151, 156, 172, 203
self-judgment, 231
service, 72, 86, 134, 159, 160, 183, 206
settlement, 236
Shechem, 143
shrewdness, 136, 137
sin, xvii, xviii, xix, xx, xxi, xxiii, 2, 10, 15, 16, 20, 21, 25, 26, 27, 28, 29, 30, 31, 32, 33, 34, 37, 38, 40, 41, 48, 57, 58, 59, 60, 63, 64, 65, 66, 67, 68, 69, 70, 71, 76, 77, 78, 79, 108, 109, 110, 111, 114, 116, 117, 123, 129, 130, 133, 136, 138, 158,159, 179, 185, 186, 193, 204
sinless life, 67
sinners, xviii, 33, 48, 59, 67, 71, 74, 123, 135, 173, 213
slave, 15, 16
smoke, 34
smoking, 34
Son of God, 43, 68, 85, 131
sonship, 56, 98, 105
Sovereign, 37
spiritual blessings, 82, 182, 184, 205, 217
spiritual gifts, 212
splendor, 72
stare decisis, 2
statutes, 2, 5, 6, 8, 18, 158

Stephen, 84, 131
submissions, 233
sufferings, 83
sun, 72, 144, 164, 182, 184
supplicant, 209
Supreme Being, 8, 11

T

tabernacle, 14, 52
Teacher, 63, 236
teachings, 13, 25, 84, 132, 179
temple, 29, 32, 52, 165, 203
temporal, 95, 105, 159, 255
temptations, 36
Ten Commandments, xix, 8, 9, 11, 12, 30
ten percent, 162, 170, 171, 179
testator, 100, 101, 102
testimony, 6, 7, 11, 41, 177, 193
thanksgiving, 151, 190, 209, 210, 211, 213, 214, 219
the Cross, 104
theology, 170, 189
throne, 47, 82, 131, 133, 219
tithes of the land, 172
tithing regime, 158, 191, 198
Transcendental, 230
transgression, xviii, xix, 7, 26, 30
treason, 33
trespass, 32

trial, 236
tricksters, 137
triumph, 66
truth, xviii, xix, xxi, xxiv, 23, 25, 29, 31, 32, 34, 36, 40, 41, 44, 45, 47, 57, 58, 59, 60, 64, 65, 66, 70, 71, 73, 78, 79, 81, 130, 151, 169, 175, 178, 191, 219

U

umpire, 27, 29, 40
understanding, 5, 139, 146, 214, 247, 254
unequal treatment, 65
Union, 140
unmerited favor, 73, 139, 153, 213

V

Vashti, 85, 147
venom, 105
victim, 62
victory, 47, 60, 185, 196
Viking, 2

W

weaknesses, 77, 221, 224, 225, 243
wealth, 51, 53, 99, 151, 152, 171, 173, 183, 219, 226
wickedness, 41, 42
wilderness, 143
William the Conqueror, 2
wine, 34, 155, 162, 166, 167, 173
wisdom, 50, 68, 110, 151, 160
womb, 164
Word of God, 70, 198, 204, 207, 215
worker, 56, 206
worship, 10, 14, 22, 52, 77, 119, 165, 175, 183
wrath, xviii, 81, 114, 123, 124

Z

Zambian, 240
Ziba, 145

www.ingramcontent.com/pod-product-compliance
Lightning Source LLC
Chambersburg PA
CBHW071143160426
43196CB00011B/1991